Animals Come to My House

Animals Come to My House

A STORY GUIDE TO THE CARE OF SMALL WILD ANIMALS

By Esther Kellner

Drawings by Heidi Palmer

G.P. Putnam's Sons • New York

To Richard Siebert, DVM, and Robert L. Stevenson, DVM,
two of the best friends any animal could have

Text copyright © 1976 by Esther Kellner
Illustrations copyright © 1976 by Heidi Palmer
All rights reserved. Published simultaneously
in Canada by Longman Canada Limited, Toronto.

Library of Congress Cataloging in Publication Data.

Kellner, Esther.
Animals come to my house
Includes index.
Summary: The author describes some of the small
wild animals she has cared for in emergencies.
Includes directions for emergency care, including
recipes for appropriate foods and instructions on
preparing the animal for a return to the wild.
1. Wild animals as pets—Juvenile literature.
[1. Wild animals as pets] I. Palmer, Heidi. II. Title
SF416.2.544   636.08′87   75-37937
ISBN 0-399-20500-4   ISBN 0-399-60990-3   lib. bdg.

PRINTED IN THE UNITED STATES

Designed by Aileen Friedman

CONTENTS

INTRODUCTION

As long as I have known the Kellners, small wild animals have been part of their household. These furry little guests might be a woodchuck, a raccoon or two, five squirrels, or three possums. None has been too young to be taken in and fed.

In addition to sharing her time and her home with orphaned or injured animals, Esther is always willing to help others with interests similar to her own. On behalf of wildlife, she has made many visits to local schools, takes part in radio and television interviews, and lectures to civic groups. She also answers telephone calls from all over the country from people seeking advice about animal care.

Those of us who share our homes with wild birds and mammals are often asked, "Why bother? Can't wild things take care of themselves?" My answer is that man has disrupted the natural environment of so many plants and animals that we have a responsibility to see that wild creatures survive. Without them, the acorns that squirrels buried and forgot about would never grow into oak trees, many ecological cycles would be broken, and the earth would become a drab and less interesting place.

When we take wild animals to care for, we are not looking for pets. Our aim is to restore them to the natural environment as soon as possible. For some animals, this might mean a few days of rest and special care. For others, it might be much longer. For example, in the wild a baby raccoon cannot care for itself, not even after it is able to eat solid food, until it has had some wilderness experience and is psychologically ready to leave its parent.

An injured animal may never be able to succeed in the wild, but if it can be properly cared for by qualified people, it can become an aid in teaching.

In this book Esther Kellner shares information that has been tested over many years and that will help small wild animals survive in a world with concerned and helpful humans.

GERTRUDE L. WARD, Ph.D.
Associate Professor of Biology,
Earlham College
Assistant Director,
Joseph Moore Museum of
Natural History

PREFACE

When we see baby animals on a TV screen, in a wildlife book, or at a zoo, we are likely to think, "How I would love to have one of those for a pet!"

But a wild animal was not created to be a pet. It belongs out of doors, "in the wild," which means in its natural home, where it can live a free life.

Baby animals in the wild do, however, become orphans sometimes. Many mothers are killed on the roads and highways; others are shot by hunters in states which have no laws to protect them while the babies are in the nest. Sometimes a tree is cut down and the mother is frightened or driven away. Or the tree blows down in a storm, killing the mother but not the little ones. Now and then, while the mother is out foraging for food, a baby animal climbs out of the nest, wanders away, and becomes lost. But it is always necessary to be sure that these small animals *are* orphans or *are* lost before trying to "rescue" them.

For almost twenty years our home has been a nursery and refuge for injured, lost, and orphaned woods babies. Most of them were brought to us by the people who found them; others were sent to us by a game warden or a veterinary for convalescent care. But there were some who barely survived long enough to reach us because the people who found them did not know what

8

to do for them. A number of tiny animals have been brought to us dying from injury, exposure, or pneumonia because the well-meaning "rescuers" did not even know that a baby animal must be warmly covered.

That is why this book has been written, not to encourage the taking of wild animals for pets, which we consider a serious wrong, but to help the kindly people who come into possession of them in a justified manner, who are willing to save a baby animal's life and care for it, according to the laws of the state, until it can go back to the wild.

The methods described are those which we have found successful and have developed, not only through observation and experience but also through consultation with naturalists, game wardens, veterinarians, and backwoodsmen.

I wish to express my thanks for the assistance of Dr. Carolyn Blakey, DVM, Animal Hospital of Richmond; Gertrude L. Ward, Ph.D., associate professor of biology, Earlham College, and assistant director of the Joseph Moore Museum of Natural History; Joseph D. Cloud, director of Indiana Department of Natural Resources; Charles D. Jones, Wayne County conservation officer; and to the two outstanding veterinarians to whom this book is dedicated: Dr. Richard Siebert, DVM, president of the Animal Hospital of Richmond, Inc., and Dr. R. L. Stevenson, DVM, director of the Stevenson Animal Hospital, associate of the Dayton Museum of Natural History. Also to my husband, Lee Kellner, and my daughter, Jamie Lee Cooper, whose dedication to the preservation of wildlife and unique rapport with animals have been of invaluable help.

Esther Kellner

Richmond, Indiana
June 24, 1975

MY SMALL
WILD ANIMALS

FIRST OF ALL

It is important to realize that any baby animal is going to require regular feedings, cleanliness, warmth, and daily care. If he needs to be fed every four hours, then he *must* be fed every four hours, day and night. If you do not feel that you can do this, then give him to someone who will not get bored with him, forget to feed him, or otherwise abuse him. This should not be just an interested friend, but someone who understands baby animals and knows what to do with them. Ask your game warden. Other persons able to help with the problem (if your state law permits) are science teachers, a zoo, a museum of natural history, a veterinarian *who has worked with small wild animals* (which some have not), or someone the veterinarian can recommend. Some states have nurseries where foundlings are taken to be properly fed and raised, and so do many zoos.

Unless you really *know* a baby animal is an orphan and too young to survive by himself, leave him where you found him. Many young animals are left alone when the mother is out foraging for her own food, but she will return to them later. Finding them alone does not always mean that they are lost or orphaned. It is extremely cruel to remove them from their natural environment without a good reason, since many of them are mishandled and most of them die.

But even if you yourself have the time, patience, and understanding necessary to bring up a baby animal, even if you come to love him very much, remember that he, like all other animals, will want a life of his own when he grows up, so be prepared to release him to the wild, where he belongs, and at the period in his life when he can adjust to it.

"Releasing Your Animal," on page 150, tells how this should be done when the time comes.

The only time we are justified in keeping a wild animal for life is when he can never take care of himself. This is sometimes true of an animal that has been crippled, has some sort of defect, or has been too long in captivity. But even then its custody must be approved by your game warden, in keeping with the state's game laws. And you can always find out about these laws by sending a letter of inquiry to your state capital, addressed to the State Wildlife Agency.

There are many laws which protect wild animals. These laws vary from state to state.

Some states will allow you to keep and raise a wild animal if you have a license. Usually this license is not expensive and is issued by the local game warden. In some states you can obtain a permit which costs nothing.

Some states will allow you to keep and raise *some* animals, but not others.

Check with your game warden to find out what the law says in your state.

14

LITTLE JOE, THE FIRST POSSUM

Of all the baby animals brought to me, he was the smallest of his kind, the weakest, and seemed the least likely to live.

A farmer and his wife had carried him in a basket from the hills of southern Indiana. They were ready to go to town that morning when they saw Sandy, their beagle puppy, carrying something around in her mouth, tossing it in the air, and catching it again. It was a baby possum. They guessed that he had wandered away from his mother and was lost when Sandy found him in the woods. Since they didn't have time to take care of him, they brought him to me.

I live, with my husband and daughter, Lee and Jamie, on the edge of Richmond, Indiana, a small midwestern city, in an area that was once a woods. It is much like living in the country, for our low rustic house is some distance from neighbors, hidden in summer by a thick growth of shrubs, hedges, bushes, and trees.

Small wild creatures are safe here, and so for several years people have brought me lost or orphaned babies. When they are old enough and strong enough to care for themselves, they find homes in our trees and garden.

I named the baby Little Joe, and as soon as he was warmed and rested, I tried to give him warm milk from a medicine dropper, but he wouldn't take it. His eyes were closed and he was very still, too weak to be afraid.

It is always important to keep baby animals warm. So I always have "animal blankets" ready for them, squares of different sizes torn from old terry-cloth towels. I laid Little Joe in a small basket with one of these blankets over him and another under him, but he stayed limp and chilly and never moved. Several times that night I looked at him, afraid that he had died. But no, he was still breathing.

The next morning I tried again to give him some whole warm milk. He opened his eyes a little and seemed hungry, but he was too weak to swallow. So I telephoned to Dr. Stevenson, a veterinarian who knows a great deal about wild animals (*which some veterinarians do not*), and he told me how to mix a strengthening formula for him. I mixed Formula 1 (see page 100) and again tried to feed him.

At first he was too weak to swallow. But whenever I picked him up, he opened his long pink mouth and snarled. This weak effort to defend himself gave me a chance to drop a little of the formula in his mouth. I did this every four hours. The next day he was stronger, also hungrier, and even licked the dropper with his long pink tongue.

After a while he stopped snarling and trying to defend himself. He seemed to recognize my scent and know that I was not an enemy. Plainly he missed the warmth and comfort of his mother's pouch, where baby possums are carried much like baby kangaroos, for he loved to be held and cuddled. Like kangaroos, Little Joe was a marsupial, an animal that carries her young in a pouch that is built into her furry middle. The possum is the only marsupial found in this country, though there are several in other countries, such as the wallaby of Australia or the Australian koala, which lives in trees and looks like a teddy bear.

He began to grow fast. Since possums are nocturnal (night) animals, he slept most of the day, warmly covered. Sometimes in the evenings, when he was wide awake, I wrapped him in one of his blankets and carried him around in the crook of my arm. When I sat down, he curled up on my lap with his tail around my wrist like a bright pink bracelet. At any sharp or unfamiliar noise, the pink bracelet tightened on my wrist. Pleased and quiet, he stared out at this new world with solemn black eyes, with no squirming or restlessness. He was not bright or curious or playful, as a puppy can be, but very interesting just the same.

Many things said about possums are untrue. Some people describe a possum's tail as long and slimy, but a possum's tail is fairly short, solid, and tapering. It is warm and dry to the touch and a little rough. Since it is a prehensile (grasping) tail, Little Joe could use it to catch hold of objects, quickly and firmly, like my finger, my wrist, the edge of his basket, anything handy. In the woods baby possums, being small and light, may hang from a branch by their tails like monkeys. But older possums are too heavy for this and will do it only in an emergency.

Little Joe was an unusually pretty possum. His white face was shaded with pale gray which blended into a darker gray around his eyes, as softly as if put on with a brush. His ears were a very dark blue. They were large, roundish, shaped like geranium leaves, and each was tipped with a line of bright pink that matched his hands, feet, nose, and tail. About three-quarters of his tail was pink, but the rest, where it attached to his body, was black. (As he grew older, the pink faded to an oyster white, as it does with all possums.)

17

Little Joe had two sets of whiskers, both long and handsome, one set on the cheeks, the other near the nose. These were "feelers," which kept him from bumping into objects after dark and which protect all animals on their night travels in search of food. His shiny dark eyes were all black because they were all pupil, which made it easy for him to see in the dark. It also made his eyes hurt in bright light.

Like most possums, he had a short, plump body which sloped toward the rear. In some ways he looked like a kitten, but was not as pretty. Instead of being smooth and soft, his fur was coarse and somewhat shaggy. The long "guard hairs" were pale and silvery, some of them tipped with black. The less black these hairs have, the whiter the animal will be, which is why all possums are not colored in exactly the same way. Some are extremely light, others a very dark gray. The belly is always lighter than the rest of the possum's body, and the head may be white or yellowish. Little Joe's head was white, but he had a yellowish patch just under his little chin. The fur close to his body was thick and oily to protect him from rain and dampness.

A young possum's fingers are always pink, but his arms are sable brown, which make him look as if he is wearing old-fashioned mitts. Since his hands have claws like those of a squirrel, he is a good climber. The hind foot, however, has a large toe with no nail which stands out away from the foot and is sometimes called a "thumb." Only three animals have such a thumb—the possum, the ape, and man. A possum's pink hand is so human in appearance, color, lines, shape that you wonder if a Gypsy could read his palm.

Some of the American Indian tribes called the possum "little whiteface." But the Spanish explorers called him "little fox" because of his fox-shaped face. The Indian name chosen by Captain John Smith was *apasum*, which gave us our word "opossum," though most people drop the first *o* when saying it.

Little Joe came to me on June 2. By June 24 he seemed strong and hearty. He had outgrown the basket that was his cradle and his baby food formula. I put a small sleeping cage on the sun porch for him and began to give him solid food, starting with scraped apple. (See page 102)

In his sleeping cage Joe had a "mattress" of thick paper towels. He slept on this all day, covered by a light cotton cloth torn from an old sheet. When the days grew hot, I removed the cloth and used it to cover and shade his eyes, so the light would not bother him. Night animals are very uncomfortable in the sunlight, and if the sun happened to be so hot that its brightness came through the cover, Little Joe would sleep with one hand over his eyes.

He had many different sleeping positions. He often slept lying on one side, with his fingers and toes gathered together into a pink bundle. One day I found him asleep with his jaws clutched between his hands, like a man who has gone to bed with a terrible toothache. One very hot day he was asleep on his back with his white front exposed and his small pink fists flung up against his cheeks.

Little Joe closed his eyes very suddenly and slept very quickly, sometimes curled up like a husky dog, nose to tail. Always his tail seemed to be a problem for him, as if he had trouble finding a resting place for it. Sometimes he curled its tip into a snail-shaped pillow and slept with his head on that. As soon as he went to sleep, his round ears "collapsed" as if they had suddenly "wilted." This "wilting" is Nature's way of keeping insects out of his ears when the possum is asleep, for an animal in the woods is often bothered by mosquitoes, ants, and gnats on hot   19 summer days. All possums, however, have very sharp ears and are quick to notice unusual sounds even when asleep. The smallest rustle of paper would make Little Joe move nervously even when he did not wake up.

Little Joe was now eating such things as grapes, cut-up apple, and small pieces of leftover chicken. Many times I sat by his cage and watched him eat. The cage was open and he was free to roam the sun porch, but he preferred to stay close to his "den" and eat his meals there. When two bits of chicken stuck together, he separated them by putting his foot on one and pulling the other free with his teeth. Since most possums are slow-witted, I was surprised to see that when Little Joe's pan was half empty, he was smart enough to tip it toward him with one hand, making the food slide his way.

Most animals, wild or tame, do not want to be bothered while they are eating and will growl, snap at, or even bite anyone who comes near them at this time. But Little Joe didn't even notice. I could pet him while he ate, even take away his food, and he would make no move to protect it. In fact, he didn't seem to know what had become of it.

I watched him closely as he ate. He held the food in one hand and took bites from it, like a child, or guided a whole piece into his mouth if the piece was small. If it was large, such as a chunk of apple, he put it in the back of his mouth and broke it into small pieces with his teeth. He then laid these neatly in front of him by hand and ate them one by one, picking them up in his fingers.

He chewed each piece solemnly and heartily for what seemed like hours. Once I watched him chew a small piece of chicken 137 times and a bite of apple 102 times.

Sometimes he ate while braced on all fours, his head boun-

cing to the rhythm of his chewing. He often stopped to get a drink of water. Possums drink a great deal of water, which is why they like to den near streams. I gave Little Joe water in a large ashtray too heavy for him to upset.

His eating was so noisy that it sometimes woke me up at night. I would hear him chewing an apple with a rapid *kish-kish-kish* sound and lapping water noisily. Yet his way of eating was very dainty. He loved Bing cherries, ate the pulp, and then neatly laid the stones in a row before him.

He would wake up about dusk and eat a small snack. Around midnight he would eat a little more, but his main meal was about five o'clock in the morning or around daylight.

Little Joe washed after eating and at other times, too—face, fingers, hands, tail—much as a kitten washes. He was so slow-witted that he might walk right through his pan of food or his ashtray of water and not even see it. But if he suddenly found himself wet or sticky, he just took another bath.

21

Little Joe yawned a great deal and surely there is nothing more amazing as the yawn of a possum. Because of his long jaws, he looked something like a crocodile at sleepy moments, and his jaws seemed wide enough to swallow his whole body. He growled quite a bit when he awoke, as if he hated to get up. And sometimes he snarled, though considering his small size, his snarls were funny instead of scary. All possums have poor eyesight, and he snarled in alarm when he heard me coming—until he got my scent.

On July 27 he first "talked" to me. I was holding him on my lap when he began making little sounds, something like the sounds of pleasure and contentment which baby squirrels make, yet not exactly the same. They were little *khik . . . khik . . . khik . . . khik!* sounds, low and rapid.

In the woods possums have an odor which can be very unpleasant. This odor is caused partly by an odd-smelling substance called musk under their skin. It is also caused by their poor eyesight and slow, blundering ways. A possum may walk right through garbage or some other mess and not even see it.

This unpleasant smell is not a fluid, as with a skunk, but is part of his defense against his enemies. He can send it out anytime he is frightened or attacked. Little Joe did this at first, but once he came to know us he stopped it, just as he stopped all the other things he did in his own defense, such as snarling, coughing, backing away, or lashing out with his tail.

It is said that possums wave their tails to frighten off enemies and that a possum, when seized, may use his tail to beat an enemy. Little Joe used to beat me like this when he didn't want me to pick him up. While he was a baby, this "beating" was hardly more than a few tiny taps, but the strong, hard tail of a full-grown possum can deliver quite a blow. His natural enemies are foxes, coyotes, bobcats, dogs, great horned owls, and, of course, man. Possums are hunted for their fur, and in some parts of the country, especially in the South, people eat boiled or roasted possums.

One day I put Little Joe down on the floor and found that he couldn't walk. He seemed suddenly weak and ill and his hind legs dragged behind him when he tried to move.

What was wrong? Had he hurt himself in some way? Possums are so awkward that they often hurt themselves in the woods, sometimes breaking a rib or a collarbone. Or perhaps Little Joe had some old injury from being so roughly treated by the beagle on the day he was brought to me. I wrapped him carefully in a soft towel and carried him to the animal hospital.

Dr. Siebert, another skilled veterinarian, examined him. He told me Little Joe's trouble was caused by a lack of certain vitamins. This often happens, he said, when baby animals are too soon removed from their mother's milk, as this milk contains the vitamins they need for strength and growth. He gave me a medicine dropper and a small bottle of liquid vitamins, much like the kind used for babies. Every day I filled the dropper to its first mark, as the doctor had directed, and squirted the liquid into Little Joe's mouth when he yawned. Most small animals dislike the cod-liver-oil flavor of this liquid, and before they will take it, it has to be thinned with water or disguised with something like orange juice. But Little Joe seemed to like it and even licked the dropper afterward. In three days he was better. In six days he was walking properly and seemed strong and well.

Little Joe was a quiet little animal, no trouble at all. He spent most of his days asleep, except when I woke him up to give him a bath. He seemed content and never lonely. Possums in the wild like to live alone and do not seem to form the friendships and loving attachments I have seen between squirrels, raccoons, and other small woods animals. As a rule, a possum travels, hunts, eats, and sleeps alone. But in very bitter winter weather several male possums or several families may huddle together for warmth in some sheltered place. It is unusual to see a grown male and female together. The father wanders away while the mother carries the babies in her pouch until they are old enough to walk along beside her or to catch a ride on her back.

Most woods animals will go to some chosen place, usually a bed of leaves, to excrete. They will not soil their nests.

A possum's chosen place is often a creek or a stream. I watched Little Joe to see when he wanted to go out, usually about midnight. I would listen to the late news on the television with Little Joe on my lap and then carry him outside.

Like a slow and poky puppy, he would wander around, sniffing and exploring every corner. He would take his time and keep in the shadows if possible, digging here and there for the grubs and insects he liked to eat. I kept a close watch so I would not lose him under a bush or in the moonlight. A possum's silvery fur blends so perfectly with moonlight that he can walk past you and never be seen unless he turns his white face toward you.

All people are interested in a possum's way of "playing dead" when he is cornered or captured. This is not a trick, however, as many people believe, but a true fainting spell. Since I have never seen a possum frightened enough to faint, I have never seen one "play dead." But many a hunter has picked up a "dead" possum by the tail and carried it away, only to find that it suddenly came to life, climbed up its own tail, and bit the hand that held it.

24

By the middle of July Little Joe was strong and well. He felt at home on the sun porch and in the garden and had learned to come and meet me when he saw me come in. We began to think about his age. Possum babies are about two and one-half months old before they can leave the mother's pouch for short periods of time. Little Joe must have left his mother and wandered too far away from her the day the beagle found him. He had been with us for about two months and now had forty-four teeth. When fully grown, he would have fifty teeth.

The time had come to release him, so that he could make his own place of grass or leaves shaped into a bed. It would be in a log, under a brush heap, or perhaps in a hollow tree or under a rock pile. Our woods area had all of these shelters. Food and drink could be found there, too. A bowl from a birdbath, placed on the ground and filled every evening, provided fresh water for our nighttime callers, which included foxes, rabbits, raccoons, flying squirrels, other possums, bats, owls, frogs, and toads, and was too heavy for them to upset. We left little snacks for them, too, including sunflower seeds for the flying squirrels, grain and pieces of apple for the rabbits, leftovers for the coons.

A possum does not travel far as long as he can find fruit, water, the grubs and insects he likes, and now and then a little meat. When I put Little Joe in his bath that day I told him, "Tomorrow night you're going out into the world. You can wander wherever you like and do exactly as you please, and you'll never, *never* have to take a people bath again!"

But we felt that he would stay near our garden, move from shelter to shelter according to the weather, come close to the house at night to eat and drink, let me pick him up and talk to him if I wished.

And he did.

SUSIE, THE SECOND POSSUM

One day a woman called to tell me about Susie, a female possum who belonged to her six-year-old boy.

"We found her lost in the woods one day when she was very tiny, and we've had her about a month. Tommy loves her, but he has a little dog that he loves, too. He can't take care of both animals, so he wants to keep the dog, but he's worried about Susie. We can't release her because she has normal sight in only one eye. Our vet said maybe you would take her and give her a good home."

We don't believe people should keep wild animals as pets, but when a case like Susie's comes up, we have to ask ourselves, "What will happen to the poor little thing if we *don't* take her?" So we said we would.

Tommy and his mother brought her to our house that afternoon. Although Tommy had decided to keep the dog, he found it hard to part with Susie. His face was red from weeping and streaked with tears. He felt better, though, when I told him he could visit her whenever he liked.

Susie was very small and dainty. Her fur was much softer than Little Joe's and almost white. A mop of soft white "hair" lay away from the center of her head in all directions. Her eyes were bright and black and showed no sign of being troubled.

There was nothing timid about Susie. She was used to having her own way and very bold about it. She was much livelier than Little Joe and very curious, even nosy. For the first hour she trotted everywhere, exploring, sniffing, and poking into things. Now and then she would climb up on my lap (or Lee's or Jamie's) as if we were old friends.

We gave her a box on the sun porch for a bed and some torn-up terry towels for blankets. Then I bathed her, just as I bathed Little Joe. Susie's bath did not please her, however, and she coughed warningly. But later she came to like warm baths and didn't want to get out of them.

Possums, even when babies, seem to know how to handle themselves in water. Once Susie climbed up and fell into a bathtub that was about half filled. Although it was the first time she had ever been in deep water, she began swimming easily, around and around, holding her nose out so she could breathe.

Susie's baths always made her sleepy, and as soon as she was dry, she would go to her bed, curl up, and sleep for hours. She spent a lot of time working with her blankets, shaping them into a round and flat nest.

Like all possums, she slept through the day and woke up at dusk. She then ate her afternoon snack, perhaps a piece of apple or some grapes, and drank a great deal of water. In the evenings we took her out of doors for exercise. It was not easy to watch over a little animal as active as Susie, especially in the dark, for she ran ahead, sniffing and exploring like a puppy. She moved back and forth with the twisty walk people call a "possum trot," stopping now and then to climb on my lap. Sometimes she would "kiss" our hands, a shivery experience, for nothing is colder than the nose of a possum. When she was quiet and content, she made a purring sound like a kitten.

Susie loved to walk and often spent most of the night walking. She would pace down the hall, up and down the sun porch, around the kitchen, stopping to look out the long windows and amusing herself in possum ways unknown to us.

It is not surprising that many an old deserted house has been considered "haunted" when possums lived in the attic or cellar or under the porch. For the noises possums make at night are *creepy!* Deep moans, mysterious coughs, strange knocks (made by clapping the tongue against the roof of the mouth), scary whimpers, and low wails. Susie made all these sounds and more, such as the loud *tsh-LOCK!* She used this sound to wake us up when she was out of water and wanted her big ashtray filled again. And when she was startled by footsteps coming toward her in the dark, she would utter a deep, low growl.

When a baby possum is born, it is smaller than a bean. In fact, twenty-four newborn possums can be put in a teaspoon! They climb into the mother's pouch at once, holding to her fur with sharp, tiny claws. The pouch has room for thirteen or fourteen babies. It contains thirteen (sometimes fourteen) tiny nipples to which the babies are attached, and since it is fur lined, it is warm and cozy. Here the little ones live and sleep and drink their mother's milk for a little more than two months. If the mother wishes to swim across a stream, she can close the pouch so tightly that the babies will not even get wet. They won't smother, either.

By the time they are two and one-half months old they go in and out of the pouch, climbing back in when scared or tired or hungry. As they grow larger and the pouch becomes crowded, some walk, some stay inside, some ride on the mother's back.

Sometimes one or two will cling to her tail with their own small tails. But pictures which show *a whole family of babies* lined up on the mother's back with their tails grasping hers are *not* correct.

Even as a baby possum, Susie had a pouch which, at first, was a tiny pink slit in the middle of her tummy. As she grew larger, it grew larger also.

She was smarter than Little Joe, came when I called her (which he never learned to do), and was always very curious about everything. Both would scratch on a door when they wanted to come in, but Susie would scratch longer and harder.

Possums don't see well, but they have excellent noses. Susie seemed to find a special scent on each of us. When she found my bedroom slippers, she would sniff them, then cuddle up to them.

Susie's walk was so slow that it was easy to laugh at her. She lifted each foot very, *very* slowly and then put it down the same way, pink toes spread wide apart. Yet possums can run quite fast when it is necessary. One night, on a country road, a possum frightened by the lights of our car ran ahead of us for some distance with a steady rapid trot, moving at fifteen miles per hour.

Like all other possums, Susie loved fruit, but aside from that her favorite foods were dry dog food, scrambled egg, and scraps of hamburger or fried chicken. Possums usually stand while they eat, but Susie often ate while sitting propped up on her thick, firm tail, as on a stool. She had another way of sitting that was surprising also, one I have never read about in any book She would sit up exactly like a cat, with her long tail wrapped around her front feet.

Little Joe was so slow-witted he would get lost in the house and could not find his way back to his cage, but Susie had no such trouble. When sleepy, she would go back to her box with her slow foot-over-foot walk, yawn a big yawn, climb in, and roll herself up in her blankets.

In the wild a possum makes his bed of leaves. He gathers them up in his mouth, passes them back under his body, and catches them in the loop of his tail. When he has a large bundle in this loop, he carries it to whatever den he has chosen, which may or may not belong to some other animal. If the owner comes back and throws him out, he doesn't seem to mind. He just ambles away and finds a new sleeping place. Once I found a possum sleeping in a squirrel house in a tree.

One fall morning I woke up to find that during the night the weather had turned chilly. And Susie had disappeared.

Finally I found her. She had become cold in the night and had moved, dragging all her blankets into a small furnace room beyond the sun porch. Here she lay, covered up and sound asleep, cozy in the furnace warmth. Both she and Little Joe disliked cold weather, and when I put them out to play in the snow, they came trotting back in a hurry. Winter weather is very hard on possums in the wild, and the cold sometimes freezes the tips of their ears or tails when they leave their dens to hunt for food.

We learned that while our wild friends liked and trusted all of us, each of them had a favorite. Susie's favorite was Lee, and she would turn to him for whatever she wanted. Only if he was not at home would she turn to me.

At two or three in the morning she would come into our bedroom to let us know that she wanted water. I would waken at the first sound of her shuffling feet on the floor, turn on my bed lamp, and find her standing on the other side of the room, gazing trustingly up at Lee. He always got up and carried her back to the sun porch, where he talked to her, petted her, and gave her fruit and water.

At night he took her for long walks in the garden when the weather was not too cold, carrying a flashlight which he used to locate her if he lost sight of her. But one night he hurried into the house and told us, "Susie is gone! I can't find her anywhere. She went under some bushes . . . and just vanished!"

Jamie and I went out to help look for her, afraid a dog might find and hurt or kill her. We searched and called, looked under bushes and in tall grass and even up into trees. Finally Lee went around to another side of the house and turned on the flashlight. At once Susie came trotting up to him, moving faster than usual. Evidently she had lost her way and was glad to see the light, knowing he was behind it.

Most creatures of the wild do not have long lives, and the life of a possum is seldom longer than two years. Susie, however,

31

lived to be a little past three. As time went on, she grew quite thin, became slower and slower, did not eat well, and sometimes seemed weak and confused. Dr. Siebert examined her and told us, "She has become a little old lady . . . very, very old."

We tried to help her but she seemed to grow weaker every day. Finally she no longer tried to walk. Instead she stayed in her bed, sometimes sleeping, sometimes sitting up and staring at the world which no longer interested her, having to be coaxed to eat and drink One day she laid down in her little blankets and never got up again.

I went in to look at her and found that she had somehow slipped out of her bed and was lying uncovered on the floor.

"Let me help you, Susie," I said.

I laid her back in her blankets, arranged them neatly, covered her warmly, and gave her some water in a medicine dropper. She drank it very slowly. A little later, Lee went in to see her, sat down on the floor beside her box, and stroked her gently. While he was stroking her, she died. We buried her in the garden near the path she liked to walk on moonlight nights, slowly and carefully, foot over foot.

SUGAR, THE GROUNDHOG

One bright spring morning a mother groundhog (or wood-chuck) took her little ones for their first walk in the meadow near their den. As the three of them moved along, nibbling fresh green grass and sniffing the fresh spring air, a passing farmer who liked to kill things raised his shotgun and shot the mother. She lay dead while her babies cried at her side and tried to awaken her.

A kindly farm woman rescued the babies and tried to bring them up, but one died and the other needed so much care that she couldn't keep it. So one day she called and asked me, "Will you take it?" I said yes and she brought the baby to us that afternoon, a furry little female about three months old.

I had always heard that groundhogs were very smart animals and very lovable There are many stories about them. One woman told me, "We once had a groundhog named Sassy. Such a baby! Always wanting love and petting. Mad if she didn't get them right away. Many a time I've seen her sit down and sulk because somebody ignored her. Or she might fly into a rage and tear up the tablecloth. They have quite a temper, you know."

It was hard to believe such stories at first, but not after we had Sugar!

33

At night she slept in a cardboard box in the basement, with old terry towels for cover. During the day she played or dozed on the sun porch or went for walks in the garden with Lee, my husband. She would trot at his heels like a puppy or nip the edge of his slacks to let him know she wanted to be picked up and carried.

She was a fat, furry little groundhog and even at the age of three months had a strong mind of her own. She expected us to be *delighted* to see her at all times, even at five o'clock in the morning. And when she wanted to be petted, she wanted to be petted now, not later, but now!

Lee was her favorite, though she was fond of all of us. When she heard me come into the house after I had been out, she knew my footsteps and came racing up from the basement to greet me. I would hear her galloping up the steps on her short, fat legs. Then . . . *bang! bang! bang!* . . . her hard nose rapped on the basement door. When I opened it, she would bounce into the kitchen and stretch her furry little arms up to me, waiting to be lifted up.

She soon learned where everything was stored, and it was hard to keep her from helping herself to whatever she wanted. *Wham!* Her quick little hands jerked open the bread drawer and she was about to jump into it to look for her favorite food, Fig Newtons. *Slam!* She opened the cabinet under the sink and snatched an English walnut from the vegetable bin there. *Slap!* She smacked the refrigerator door with her plump black hand, demanding lettuce. *Bang!* on the sink cabinet, wanting a drink.

Above all things she loved peanut clusters We let her have one very small cluster a day, and she knew just where to look for it. She never forgot that Lee kept a bag of these candies in the third drawer of a maple chest in our bedroom.

Every morning, around daylight, Sugar raced up the basement steps, knocked loudly, and bounced in when I opened the door. This time she gave me no greeting, for her mind was on the peanut cluster. With thudding feet, she streaked to the bedroom and began pulling at Lee. Then she ran to the chest, lifted herself on her hind legs, and seized the knob of the third drawer. Like a doting father, Lee got up and gave her the peanut cluster. She then sat up at the foot of the bed and ate her treat.

But she was not always in such a happy mood, for she did have a quick temper. If I took some forbidden object away from her or if I refused to let her do something, she would fly into a rage. First she gave me an angry look. This was followed by an angry stamping of her front feet. Then she spread her short, stubby tail until it looked like a small, shaggy fan. This tail was about the size and shape of a shaving brush.

Then she would rush at me with an angry cry, trying to nip my ankles or tear my clothes. She would seize whatever was handy, Lee's trouser cuff, the hem of my skirt, the edge of a dish towel, or anything she could rip and pull. No wonder the woman said her groundhog would tear up the tablecloth!

When Sugar came to us, she was wrapped in a big, much-washed olive-colored towel left over from somebody's army service. She clung to this towel as some children cling to a baby blanket. She slept with it every night and often took it with her, dragging it along with one corner of her mouth. If I put her back in her box to punish her for something, she would sit there sulking and glaring, with the edge of this towel in her teeth.

Sometimes she sulked like a dog, pretending not to see me and looking the other way. (We have also seen our fox squirrels do this.) If I tried to make up with her or pet her, she would jerk away from my hand with a sharp *mirrrrrrrr!*

35

Yet she loved to romp with me and her favorite game was one we called Blanket. I would roll her up in a small blanket and slide her across the kitchen floor, which she considered great fun. Sometimes she would scurry out and seize one corner of the blanket and we'd have a tug-of-war with it. She played much as a puppy plays, but her teeth and nails were so sharp that it was safest to play with her when I could stop her merry charges with a blanket, like a bullfighter.

Groundhogs, we learned, are proud, independent, stubborn, curious, smart, lovable, and always busy. Their burrows, which they dig deep under the ground, are quite large—three rooms, three hallways, a back door, and a front "patio."

The front hall, which is quite long, reaches to the bedroom, where the groundhog sleeps, builds her nest, and has her babies. A shorter hallway leads to the toilet. The back door is a second hole (or entrance) carefully hidden in brush or bushes. By sticking her head up through this hole, Mrs. Groundhog can see what is going on in her neighborhood, which helps her to be aware of dogs and strangers. If an enemy starts in her front door, she can escape out the back. Her eyes, nose, and ears are all close to the top of her head, which means that she can see, smell, and hear without really being seen. Her little black hands, which are very strong, look as if they are covered with black leather gloves. And because she uses her nose for digging, it is very hard.

The "patio" at her front door is a mound of dugout earth smoothed into a comfortable shape. Here she can lie down, rest, watch the neighborhood, doze and sun herself, or watch her children while they play. All groundhogs like to take sunbaths.

A female groundhog is a busy housekeeper. She works at her hallways, keeping them clean and neat. To do this she lies on her side and uses her nose to push out trash like pebbles and twigs. She cleans her bedroom and changes the bed, carrying out the old and dead grasses which have been her mattress, bringing in fresh and fragrant ones. She carries waste from the toilet or perhaps seals it up behind a wall of fresh dirt. She keeps her doorways open and ready for escape, but well hidden. When she isn't busy housekeeping, she is busy hunting for food, usually plants found in her dooryard.

At first we cleaned Sugar's box for her, but this did not seem to please her. Plainly, she wanted to do it herself. She would work busily for hours, cleaning out the old paper on which she had slept, bringing in new. She tore newspaper into bits, carried them into the box, and arranged them to suit herself. Since she liked to sleep on cloth, we gave her old towels, freshly washed, nearly every day. But she might seize and steal anything else that pleased her—napkins, dish towels, even shirts—until we hid the laundry baskets. For toilet use she had a box of sand that was odorless and clean.

A groundhog needs more than one den to feel safe, so Lee brought Sugar a second cardboard box and put it in a different corner of the basement. The first thing she did was make a "back door" by ripping a crooked circle out the back, near the top. At the slightest sound on the basement steps, her little head would pop out, so that she could see who or what was coming.

Besides the indignant *mirrrrr!* Sugar made little barking sounds of excitement when we played games with her. Sometimes she would whistle for attention. (All groundhogs can whistle.) But the sound she made most often was a happy one, a low, liquid, burbling sound like blowing bubbles through a water pipe. She would follow Lee with this burbling sound and he would tell her, "Sugar, you've left your motor running."

One of the things she liked best was the rocking chair on   37

the sun porch. It gave her a wonderful view of the neighborhood, which would please any groundhog, and she spent hours
there, looking out the long windows and rocking slowly back
and forth.

Groundhogs hibernate in winter and sleep in their dens for
months, usually until spring. They begin to prepare for the winter early in the fall or even in late summer.

By the first of September Sugar seemed able to think of nothing else. One morning her busy little hands snatched out the cold-air register in the living room, and I came in just in time to see her disappear down this ready-made tunnel. I coaxed her out with a piece of banana, which she loved, and kept her away from the furnace passages after that, even though no fire was burning.

One day I went out to the garden to pick some marigolds. When I came back, I found that Sugar had pulled the bread drawer out of the cabinet, laid the wrapped loaves neatly on the kitchen floor, dragged a dish towel into the drawer, and was sound asleep in this brand-new den. As usual, she was snoring loudly.

Now when Lee took her for a walk, she went straight to a bank near the street and started to dig into it. When a groundhog digs, the dirt flies. But Nature has given him ears which he can close whenever he wishes, and this keeps the dirt from bouncing into them. Sugar would dig into the hillside very fast, then turn around in the little tunnel she had made and push the dirt out, working by instinct, since she had never seen anybody dig anything.

Soon, however, she left this tunnel, which was now about three feet long, as if to look for a better place. She seemed determined to cross the street, so Lee carried her across to see what it was that she wanted to do there. She marched straight through the garden of our neighbor, Mrs. Griffis, and out to an old carriage house. Here she explored everything very closely, but made no effort to dig and seemed satisfied when Lee carried her home again.

With the coming of early fall, Sugar began to eat everything in sight and beg for more. She ate and ate and *ate*. She grew   39 fatter and fatter and *fatter*, for groundhogs, like bears, store up fat for their long winter sleep. Somehow she knew that before she went into her winter den, she must be much, *much* fatter. So she stuffed herself until she could hardly waddle. For if hibernating animals are too thin, they will wake up too early—even in winter—and suffer, perhaps die, for lack of food. Sometimes, during a warm spring, a groundhog may wake up too soon, but if he can find a few green plants, he can eat them and then go back to sleep unharmed.

Deep in his den, the groundhog seems hardly alive. As he sleeps, his temperature falls, his heartbeat becomes slow, and he takes only one breath in six minutes instead of the forty he takes when awake.

Groundhogs don't like to use the same den for winter that they used in summer. Summer dens are usually tunnels near open fields or meadows, close to tasty plants and vegetables. In winter such a den is not safe, for the shrubs and bushes that hid it are now bare, and a groundhog going in and out is easily seen. Also a den in the open is not as warm as a den in a sheltered place. So a groundhog often makes a winter home in woods or under an old abandoned building.

As the days grew crisp and frosty, Sugar became more and more restless. She would pace up and down the sun porch, push at the doors, sniff at the windows, and act as if she had forgotten us altogether. Then one afternoon I heard a crashing sound in the region of the sun porch, where she had been rocking and looking out. When I went to see what had happened, the rocking chair was empty and Sugar was gone. She had torn the screen away with her sharp little claws and squeezed herself through the glass louvers. It was hard for me to believe she could do this, yet I know that many wild animals have the ability to "squeeze themselves small" in order to go through very narrow spaces.

I went out to look for her but there wasn't a sign of her. Jamie helped me search the lawn and garden, and when Lee came home all three of us looked, calling Sugar all the while. We left the sun-porch door open that night and went to look for her every time we heard a noise.

But she did not come back.

Now that she was as round as a basketball, she was ready to curl up in her den until spring. We felt that this den would be somewhere in the neighborhood, but where? Then we thought of Mrs. Griffis' garden, which Sugar had found so interesting, but it showed no signs of digging.

"Still, I think you'll see a little groundhog here next spring," Lee said. "If you do, please call us." Mrs. Griffis said she would.

Winter passed. It was a very cold winter and Lee worried about Sugar but I did not, for I knew she was smart and could take care of herself.

"Wherever she is, she is nice and warm," I told him. For a groundhog's den is snug, well above water and dampness. And I had a feeling that she would come back.

In February people began saying, "She'll be coming out soon. Groundhog Day, you know."

It is surprising how many people really believe that on February 2 every groundhog opens his eyes and comes out to look at the weather. They seem to forget that this is an old superstition.

An old European superstition said that if a badger came out of his den and saw his shadow on February 2, there would be six more weeks of winter. Early pioneers in this country (living in areas where badgers were not seen) transferred this fancy to the groundhog because of his resemblance to the badger in home and habit.

41

Most groundhogs come out of their dens in March. The male groundhogs come out first and start traveling from den to den in search of a mate. The female hears the male at her door and wakes up. If she doesn't like his looks, she chases him away. But if he pleases her, she lets him come in and they live in her nice neat tunnel until they have babies. The father, however, takes no part in bringing them up and usually leaves before they are born.

"Maybe Sugar has found a mate and doesn't intend to come back," Lee said.

But I didn't think so. It seemed unlikely that there would be another groundhog nearby. These animals do not range far from their first homes and are almost never seen in town.

On April 10 I heard a noise near the basement window about daylight, when groundhogs often feed. So Lee put some pieces of apple there, and next morning they were gone. Still, a possum or a raccoon or a hungry rabbit could have taken them.

Then, on April 12, the gardener working on Mrs. Griffis' lawn reported, "There's a groundhog sunning itself out by the big rock."

Lee hurried across the street carrying an English walnut and a banana. The moment she heard his footsteps on the grass, the groundhog disappeared. Then Lee saw that a small, secret tunnel had been dug between two rocks and led back under the old carriage house. The entrance was so small he had not even noticed it until now and would not have believed that Sugar could get into it.

Leaning down to it, he called her name. There was a short pause. Then a black nose and two wary eyes appeared. He held out the food and she took it eagerly, but backed away with it.

Lee leaned closer to the hole and spoke quietly. "Sugar, I'm going home now. If you want to go with me, come on."

While the gardener stared in astonishment, she came out of the den and trotted after Lee, just as if she had understood every word. At the edge of the garden Lee picked her up and carried her across the street.

No world wanderer ever had a heartier or more loving welcome. Since there were no males to awaken her, she had slept a very long time. She was still stiff-legged, shaky on her feet, and didn't seem to be fully awake even now. Of course she didn't know she had been gone such a long time.

In the basement her favorite towel lay washed and folded. The moment I gave it to her, she seized it in her teeth and dragged it to her box in the far corner. Then she became very busy, bringing in blankets and tearing up paper to line her bed. All the time, she worked with an air of impatience, like a fussy old lady, as if she were thinking, I just *knew* I'd come home and find everything in a mess!

She was very thin now, hungry and thirsty. After she had drunk fresh water from her dish, she ate nuts, grapes, pieces of pear, and her favorite, a fig bar.

For a while she followed at Lee's heels, burbling her odd sound of contentment. Then she went out on the sun porch and rocked in the rocking chair. After dark she returned to the basement, pulled her towel over her head, and went to sleep. We tiptoed down to look at her, so glad to have her safe at home.

But Sugar was no longer content to stay indoors all day and go outside only in the evening. She had known freedom. She wanted to explore the garden whenever she wished, go in and out as she pleased, nibble any fresh green plants she might find, and climb the trees. The redbud and sweet gum trees were her favorites. She would climb up as high as she wanted to go, look around for a while, and then come down the trunk backward.

Every evening she expected us to take the time to play with her. Like most woods pets, groundhogs get very excited when they are romping or playing and may bite too hard, but a sharp spank usually teaches them to become more careful. A mother raccoon often teaches disobedient babies in this way. With Sugar, however, the method didn't work.

One evening when she was being too rough, Lee gave her a small spank. At once she stopped playing, drew back, and stared at him. The expression of a little groundhog can tell a great deal about its feelings. Now Sugar looked surprised and then hurt.

With great dignity, she "drew herself up tall" and turned her head away. When Lee tried to talk to her, she acted as if she didn't hear him. Later, when he tried to pet her and feed her, she would not even look at him. When he touched her, she jerked away with a sharp *mirrrrr!* as if saying, "Leave me alone!" Almost three days went by before she would make up with him. There are other wild animals, such as the wolf, that have this kind of pride and may never forgive a person for striking them even lightly.

Whenever Sugar showed signs of wanting to cross the street, Lee would carry her across and leave her in the Griffis garden, where she scurried happily into her den under the carriage house. Here she would stay until we came back for her in the late afternoon.

That summer Lee was ill and in the hospital. While he was away, I would go across the street at five o'clock to bring Sugar home. She came with me, but not very willingly. She didn't want me to carry her, she wanted Lee. She hunted him in all the rooms, in the garden, the basement, everywhere. One evening when I went to get her, she would not come. She knew that Lee wasn't at home, so she stayed hidden inside her den, and the next day she set out to hunt for him, as she so often did when he was out of doors.

It was a summer day, burning hot, and I was sure that Sugar would be needing water. I went to the carriage house and called her, but there was no answer and no glimpse of a little groundhog face peeping out. I called again and again, but she did not come, and after a while I realized the den was empty.

I did not know where she had gone and was afraid she was in danger. A groundhog in town is an unusual sight, and there are people who will club or even kill an unusual animal, as cruel and senseless as this may be. Other people who had never seen a groundhog closely might be afraid of her, perhaps hurt her. Or a dog might chase her. . . .

I called the radio stations and asked them to announce that a tame groundhog had been lost and to call my number if she was seen. But no one should try to capture her, for if she became frightened, she might bite.

The day grew hotter and hotter. That afternoon, five blocks from our house, a man and his wife were working in their garden. For some reason they had left a side door open.

Down the street came a hot and tired little groundhog. Seeing the open door, she went inside, just as she did at home. It was nice and cool inside, so she lay down in front of the air conditioner with all four feet in the air and went to sleep.

When the man and his wife came in, they were more than a little astonished to find this strange animal asleep in their house. Not knowing what else to do, they called the police.   45

The police arrived just as Sugar woke up. She was curious about the officers and pleased when they petted her, so she let them lift her into a box and put her in the police car. They drove to a park about two miles away and let her out on a woodsy hillside.

We never saw her again.

Since she was carried away in a closed box and could not see where she was being taken, she probably could not find her way back. Of course I went to the park as soon as I heard what had happened and called her again and again. Lee went, too, after he came home, thinking his voice might bring her. But there was no answering rush of little feet, no excited burble, no merry face.

We were aware that the time had come to return her to the wild, but we had planned to release her in some carefully chosen spot between woods, meadow, and stream in early July. We knew, however, that the park bordered on meadows, had streams and springs, and was large enough to shelter a number of groundhogs. Also the director did not object.

So we are sure that Sugar found another secret place and dug another den. Perhaps a male groundhog woke her up the next spring and she took him for her mate. Perhaps she has little ones now. We wanted her to have a life of her own in the world from which she came, but we still miss her. She was the most intelligent little animal we ever had and one of the most endearing.

LITTLE BIT, THE CHICKAREE SQUIRREL

One early-spring day when I was walking in the woods, I sat down to rest with my back against an old tree. While I was sitting there, I had the feeling that something was watching me, which would not be unusual, for when you walk in the woods, many eyes are on you. Squirrels peer at you from nests and holes and branches. A chipmunk stops under a bush to watch you. A groundhog peeps from the back door of his tunnel. A fox looks out of his den. And there are always birds to see you and scream in alarm to the whole woods. *"Stranger coming! Stranger coming!"* Especially warning birds, such as crows and bluejays.

I felt that someone was watching me from behind, and so I began to turn my head slowly, and even more slowly, until I could see the tree trunk. And there, perched on the bark a little way above my head, was one of the prettiest little creatures in all the woods—a chickaree.

A chickaree is a tiny squirrel. Of the several kinds of red squirrels, the chickaree is the smallest and most beautifully colored. In spite of his size, he is very bold and is well-known for his temper tantrums and his curiosity. No wonder he was watching me with such interest now. Judging from his age (very young), I thought I might be the first human he had ever seen.

Suddenly he gave a sharp whistling sound, *whist!* and another little chickaree appeared. Now I could see the location of their nest, though it was so well hidden that I would never have seen it at all if the second little squirrel hadn't looked out of it. In the trunk of the tree there was a split about three feet long, and though it was hardly more than a crack, some dry grasses were sticking out of it. Behind this crack was the chickaree nest.

Now the second squirrel came out and moved down the tree trunk in my direction, but very carefully in case I should be dangerous. He looked and I looked, scarcely daring to blink my eyes. Suddenly he cried, *"Whist!"* and shot back up the tree.

This was a call to the rest of the family. It must have meant something like, *"Come here! Come quick! Come and see!"* For two more little chickarees came out of the nesting crack and looked at me. Now there were four, all staring with large black eyes. None of us moved. It was so funny I had to smile, and when I did, they knew I was something that could move.

Whist! It was the same whistle, but in another tone. This time it was an alarm. All four shot into the nest with the speed of a rocket. As I got up and walked away, one stuck his tiny head out long enough to sass me. *Brrrrrrrrr!*

A few days later a woman telephoned me and said she had found a baby squirrel. She wanted me to come and look at it and tell her how to take care of it. I was much surprised by the call because it was now October, which is much later than squirrels are usually born. When I saw the tiny creature, I was even more surprised. It was a baby chickaree.

She had not known that baby animals must be kept warmly covered and had laid it in an open box, where it was almost dead from cold and hunger. She had found it on the sidewalk the evening before. No doubt it had fallen from its nest onto the grass and leaves and had crawled out to the sidewalk searching for its mother. We tried to find the nest or the mother, but saw no sign of either one.

When I told her the baby would have to be fed every three hours, she asked me to adopt him, for she worked in an office and could not take care of him. So I covered him warmly and brought him home. Jamie named him Little Bit.

We decided that he was about a month old, since his eyes were open, but he was still so tiny we hardly dared hold him for fear of hurting him. At the time he weighed only an ounce. Even after he was fully grown, he weighed only four ounces and could stand on all four feet on the palm of Jamie's small hand. His own hands (or front feet) were about as large as the head of a kitchen match.

We examined him carefully, wondering at his beauty. His eyes were large, round, and shiny black, each rimmed in white. His coat was a dark reddish color, smooth and gleaming like a polished table. His underparts were snow white, divided from the reddish top by a sharp black line. His small tail was flat, like a yellowish feather edged in black. One of the most interesting things about him was his ears. They were long and stood straight up, with little tufts of fur growing around them. The ears themselves were so transparent that when you held him up to the light, tiny veins like the veins on a leaf could be seen running through them.

Though he was very weak, he flew into a temper and complained loudly when we handled him, for chickarees complain about everything. He complained when we fed him, covered him, looked at him.

His mouth was too tiny for a bottle, so we fed him with a medicine dropper while he was on the formula. At first we gave him only a few drops, since he needed very little to fill his tummy. He ate every three hours and slept a great deal afterward. During this time we kept him covered, but as he gained strength, he would sit up in his blankets to see what was going on. We then started offering him one teaspoon of formula at each feeding, but he did not always take all of it. Unlike most squirrels, he never seemed to want more than was good for him.

A pet squirrel will choose for himself the person he wants to belong to, no matter who may be his rescuer. And in a short time we could see that Little Bit had chosen Jamie. He soon looked to her as his mother. When he wanted food or attention, he would whistle for her to come. *Whist! Whist! Whist!* When he heard a strange noise or saw a strange visitor, he would give a shrill alarm cry, *brrrrrrr!* which sounded somewhat like the call of a locust.

He never "talked" to me, but when Jamie fed him or played with him, he made little contented sounds—*mm . . . mm . . . mm*. And sometimes when he was pleased he made a high-pitched sound something like a thin whine. *Mmmmmmmmmmmmm!*

As soon as he was old enough to be taken off his milk formula, we started to feed him a cereal mixture, which made him furious when it stuck to his chin. He liked the cereal, but hated being sticky and flew into a regular tantrum if a drop fell on him. Jamie would carry him to the bathroom and wash the stickiness off his face with a wet cottonball, which made him scream and kick with rage. But he never tried to bite her because no woods animal bites its mother except in play.

At this time Little Bit was so small that he held to Jamie's hand by wrapping his arms and legs around her first finger. His

50

tantrums were very funny. He would glare at us, his little ears bristling, the furry tufts on his jaws sticking out, and he would squall angry protests in his own language.

I would ask, "What do you suppose he is saying?"

And Jamie would answer, "I think he means: *Stop getting me all gooey or I'll leave home!*"

When he was about six weeks old, we brought an empty birdcage from the attic and put him in that, which seemed to make him happy, because it was circular in shape and he could race around it as much as he pleased. Jamie added animal blankets and he shaped these into a burrow where he hid when things got too noisy for him, which was often. Even the sound of high heels passing by annoyed him.

A week or so later Jamie started taking him out of the cage to play. He would spring to her shoulder, then race around and around her, as a squirrel races around the trunk of a tree. It was a sort of hide-and-seek, catch-me-if-you-can game. He would suddenly appear at her ear. When she saw him, he would cry, "*Whist!*" and run around to her other side and pop up under her arm, all the time with a grin on his little face.

As he grew older and stronger, he learned to leap to the floor. Then he would run around the room at such a high speed that he was only a streak. This worried Jamie. She was afraid he might disappear into some little niche where she couldn't find him.

After he discovered that he could run, he began to take long leaps, very long for an animal his size. He was beautiful in flight, with his flat tail spread out to balance him and his arms as stiff as a dancer's. He would sail from Jamie's arm to the bookcase, back to her shoulder and then to her desk, all the time crying out, "*Wist! Whist! Whist!*" 51

Once he leaped into an open desk drawer among pencils, erasers, paper clips, and other things. He ran all the way through it, fell out the space at the back, tumbled to the floor and bounced up in a rage. *Brrrrrrr!* As if to say, "Why did you let that happen to me?"

Of all the animals we have sheltered, he was the most "touchy." Of course, because he was tiny and pretty and appealing, everyone wanted to see him. But he didn't want strangers looking at him. When they came near he would cover his eyes and make whimpering sounds.

We knew that every living thing has to have a "safety zone" around it, a certain amount of space which he needs to make him feel comfortable. Jamie began to feel that Little Bit's "safety zone" was larger than the birdcage, so she moved him to a parakeet flight cage, which was large and roomy. This made him happy, and he ran around and around it, whistling his delight.

We built "furniture" for the new cage, apple and maple twigs which formed ladders and resting places up and down the walls. One branch was hung loosely from the top so that Little Bit could swing on it.

People who came to our house always wanted to see our animals and, in spite of our warnings, were always poking a finger into their cages, which frightened them. To any creature as tiny as Little Bit, somebody's forefinger looked as large as a python, and he felt that he had to defend himself. Chickarees are very brave and bold. They have been known to attack a fox, even a grown man. So when a woman poked her finger at Little Bit one day, he bit it. His tiny teeth were finer than sewing-machine needles and could bite about as fast as a sewing machine sews.

When he was fully grown, Jamie put him in a little basket

(the kind used for party favors) and weighed him on my postal scales. Four ounces. He looked strong and healthy and had always been very lively, but suddenly he became ill.

I heard him whimpering and called Jamie. When she reached into the cage he crawled into the palm of her hand and lay there making a sobbing sound. We didn't know what was wrong with him and it was impossible for a veterinarian to examine him, even Dr. Siebert, who had visited him many times. He wouldn't let anyone touch him but Jamie.

For days he was quiet, so quiet that his little nails had no chance to be worn down and became very long. One night Jamie found him huddled on top of his covers, his eyes full of pain. He had caught one long nail in his blanket and almost torn it off. We treated it with a spray-on antiseptic and it soon healed, but he was still weak and ill.

53

Dr. Siebert reminded us that baby animals raised by humans usually have a vitamin lack because they have been deprived too early of their mother's milk. He suggested giving Little Bit the vitamin drops we used for the other animals. Jamie diluted this with water and poured it into the ashtray used for his water dish. Because he would eat almost anything that was sweet, she added a bit of honey, and his little tongue soon lapped up this remedy.

In a few days he was better. In three weeks he was much better, and in a month he was running as fast as ever, insulting our visitors as sharply as usual, and going *whist*! when he wanted Jamie.

He was a fine little "watch squirrel," for no sound, however soft, escaped his perky ears. His cage was near the patio door and when the curtains were closed at night, he could not see outside. Yet in the middle of the night he might sound an alarm, *brrrrrrr!* Jamie or I would look out and see a possum walking across the patio. How he could have heard this soft-walking animal was hard to understand! On summer nights a possum has passed right by me and I heard him only because he blundered into some dry leaves.

Little Bit was a great hoarder, for it is the nature of these animals to have what is called a midden. This is something like an apartment where they live and store all their belongings. In the wild they may have a midden in their nest and one or two middens on the ground.

For his first midden Jamie gave Little Bit a short piece of drapery material, old and soft, and he spent several days getting it shaped just right. He tugged it here and there, working very hard, making a number of tunnels in the cloth by patting them into place with his tiny hands. Until the midden was finished and filled, he was too busy to play. But once it was done, he wanted Jamie to see it and called to her in a bossy manner, *"Whist! Whist!"*

When she put her hand in the cage and examined the midden, he did not seem to mind, though I'm sure he would have flown into a rage if anyone else had touched it.

There was a "front hall" where nothing was stored. ("A place to leave your coat and boots, I guess," Jamie said.) There was a tiny room holding walnut pieces. Beyond that was a room full of sunflower seeds and then a small bedroom. All these came off a central tunnel, or "hallway." Beyond the bedroom was a room full of shelled corn, and at the end of the tunnel a small opening led to the "bathroom," a piece of torn-up tissue in one corner of the cage. Everything was neatly arranged and in its proper place.

While Jamie examined it, Little Bit ran along beside her hand making excited clicking sounds. We didn't always know what the animal sounds meant and sometimes had to use our imaginations. "I think," said Jamie, "he's so proud of the midden he wants to show it to me . . . and he's afraid I'm going to miss something."

As her hand was lying in the "front hall," Little Bit seized a piece of Kleenex and began packing it around her wrist, bustling, "talking" all the time, as if he thought she had come to stay and was trying to store her, too.

Little Bit often stored some of the food he didn't eat and when grapes or bits of apple started to spoil, the midden had to be cleaned out. That didn't please Little Bit at all. While Jamie washed the cage and cleaned the midden, he would watch from the swing and whimper. He whimpered like a child, with his tiny fists in his eyes. She told me she thought this must mean:

"Look what you're doing! Throwing out all we've got for winter! We'll starve, that's what we'll do, starve!" She always saved the best of his stores, though, and added new ones, so he was soon busy building another midden and making new rooms.

He never tried to quarrel with her or bite her when she cleaned his cage, since the tie between them was so strong that when she went to Indiana University in the summer, he sat and whimpered and refused to eat. Now and then he would look hopefully around, calling a sad "Whist!"

One day while she was gone and I was trying to give him some fresh water, he got out of his cage. At the same moment Sugar, the groundhog, came out on the sun porch. Little Bit had never seen a groundhog and she had never seen a chickaree. They stopped and stared at each other as if to ask, "What on

earth is *that?*" Lee and I hurried up, afraid one might hurt the other, but this didn't happen. Instead Little Bit pranced forward and then away, as if inviting Sugar to romp. In another moment they were going around and around the room in a sort of catch-me-if-you-can game, both grinning broadly. It was a surprising and appealing sight, and the companionship helped Little Bit to feel better about Jamie's absence.

Sometimes Susie Possum went into the room where he lived and he would stretch up in his cage, almost on tiptoe, watching her. He was very curious about her, but didn't want her to come near and would scold her with a noisy *brrrrrrrr!* as she ambled past. All chickarees are good at scolding other animals, especially any that come near the midden. They grind their teeth, jerk their tails, stamp their tiny feet, chirr and scream and jeer.

But people who have observed chickarees closely know that as a family they seem to have a gentle affection for one another. In a litter of young (sometimes as many as seven or eight) there seems to be a close "family feeling," and though they are quarrelsome by nature, they never seem to quarrel with one another. They nestle together fondly, and if one leaves the nest to look at the world, the others seem worried and restless until he is safely back again.

Little Bit seemed to consider Jamie his "family," and when she tried to release him, he would not go. We thought he would make a home in one of our trees, but instead he kept coming back and clinging to the screen, whimpering to be let in. At last Jamie decided to let him stay, fearing he would die if she did not.

Little Bit lived almost seven years. As he grew older, his little face grayed around the muzzle, like the face of an old dog. He became very grouchy and seemed to grow stiff in his joints, as if he had rheumatism.

In his old age he still whistled for Jamie, but his *whist!* was less strong and shrill now. Sometimes when a raccoon climbed the tree outside his door at night or a possum paced across the patio in the dark, he did not give even a small alarm. But he still wanted Jamie to reach in and pet him, and he sniffed happily when she put cologne on her fingers, for all squirrels like flower scents.

He was a "little old man" now, and his strength was failing. One morning when she heard no sound from him, she found him lying quiet in his bed. He had died in his sleep.

The other day she told me, "I buried him in the garden nearly three years ago. But sometimes I find I'm still listening for his alarm call and his little whistle."

CEECEE, THE RACCOON

One afternoon a man came to our house carrying a basket. In it were three small black creatures, the largest about the size of a lipstick.

"They're baby coons," he told me.

This was on Sunday. On the Friday before, the family had heard a scratching sound in the chimney and decided that some wild creature had fallen into it and couldn't get out. The father climbed to the roof and lowered a rope. In a short while a young female raccoon climbed out and ran away.

On Saturday they again heard sounds in the chimney, but very feeble sounds. On Sunday they explored the fireplace with a flashlight and found the three babies that had been lying in the soot and cold, uncovered and unfed, for nearly three days.

As with fox-squirrel litters, the babies seem to come in three sizes, small, medium, and large. Small and Medium were so quiet that at first I thought they were dead. But Large was a tiny bundle of angry babyhood, squalling loudly for food and trying to crawl around and find it.

Using a dry cloth, we wiped the soot from the babies, warmed them, and tried to feed them. But cold, hunger, and   59 neglect had been too much for Small and Medium, and they died that night. I think they were born as the frightened mother tried to claw her way out of the chimney and she never saw them.

Only Large was left now, but we could see that even in his starved condition he had strength and spirit. At first we fed him with a medicine dropper, but he soon refused to take his formula this way and drank it greedily from a bottle. We fed him with a special, small pet bottle, but some people have used a baby bottle successfully. As he nursed, he instinctively pushed his little hands outward, something a baby raccoon does to force the milk from the mother's breast and increase the flow.

Large was still small, exactly the length of my forefinger, which is two and three-quarter inches long. His fur was dark gray, for raccoons are furred when they are born. His tail, hardly bigger than a toothpick, was already circled with tiny rings. His little face already showed the pattern of a mask.

I fed him at first with warm water sweetened with a bit of honey: 3/4 cup of water mixed with 1/4 teaspoon of honey or white Karo. After that I gave him his own formula. (See page 118)

Books about raccoons often say: "These animals are very stubborn and if they cannot have their own way when they are grown, they may become dangerous."

Already Large acted as if he were doing his best to become dangerous. He squalled as if in rage when his bottle was late, shook his tiny fists, kicked and tumbled. He had a huge appetite, and we were afraid of overfeeding him, something which causes the death of many small foundlings. He howled for his bottle every hour on the hour so we let him have it, but gave him only a very small amount of the formula. Later he was placed on a three-hour schedule.

In a week his thin fur was covered by a thicker and lighter

growth, soft and fluffy. His mask grew darker and gave him the look of a tiny bandit. He seemed surprisingly strong for a week-old baby, especially one which had such a starved beginning. But already he had learned to crawl, was trying to walk, and squalled furiously when he fell over.

In his warm basket he slept soundly, curled up into a ball. He was so little that Lee could hold him in one palm, with plenty of room to spare. The three of us took turns getting up at night to feed him, holding him with one hand while he nursed. This was different from the nursing habits of other woods babies we had had. He would open his mouth (which seemed amazingly large and bright red), take some milk, then lean back and let it run down his throat.

Sometimes, like a human baby, he would fall asleep while he was nursing.

Large's eyes were still closed, and we did not expect them to open for at least two weeks. (Most raccoons open their eyes when they are twenty days old.) We would put him back in his blankets, cover him gently, and tiptoe away. But raccoons are smart animals and he soon learned that a footstep might mean food, so he yelled at the top of his voice when we came near or passed by.

A baby raccoon cries like a human baby, in the same tone, in the same way, but his voice is very tiny. Five months must pass before he is weaned, during which he cries a lot even when he is full. Jamie groaned as she counted on her fingers. "August! He'll be crying like this until August!" His crying tapered off, along with his need for so many feedings, but he still cried like a human baby when he was hungry.

All little raccoons cry a lot. Often when the mother raccoon takes them for a walk, they will follow behind her, yelling

"Waaa! Waaa! Waaa!" like children who want to be picked up and carried. A mother raccoon is strict with her young, for their lives depend on obeying her commands. When they disobey or pay no attention to the lessons she is trying to teach them, she will punish them by nipping their noses sharply and may give them a spank or two.

About this time we decided that we could not go on calling our little raccoon Large, so we started calling him Coon-coon. Later we just used the initials C.C. and called him Ceecee.

When he was two months old, he looked much like a kitten or perhaps more like a tiny lion cub. The rings on his tail were blacker than before and so was his mask. His eyebrows and the tips of his ears were white. The ears were standing up now, though at first they had been flat against his head. He was still on the bottle, but had begun to make clumsy hand-washing motions at mealtime.

He slept less and less and spent a good deal of time just looking around. After his eyes were open, he started playing with the objects around him. Sometimes he would lie on his back and play with his feet, just like a human baby.

Ceecee seemed to grow smarter every day. He knew Jamie's voice and would come when she called him. She took him out of the basket and put him in a small but roomy cage. Ceecee examined the latch closely with his little hands, then snapped it open and walked out. We learned later that raccoons can also slide bolts, untie knots, open canisters, bottles, boxes, and cupboards.

Now he was no longer clumsy and awkward, but cuddly and active. We let him play around the house for exercise, and Jamie began taking him out of doors on warm fall days. He liked to look around, but was afraid of the grass and cried when

she put him down on it. When frightened, he would climb up her slacks as fast as he could go to get back in her arms.

At this time Jamie still had Little Bit, the chickaree squirrel. When he saw her carrying Ceecee, he shouted angrily, *"Brrrrrrrrrrrrrrr!"* After that she would sneak the little raccoon past the jealous chickaree by hiding him under her jacket.

At the age of nine weeks Ceecee had four teeth, two lower ones all the way through and two upper ones coming in. All four were very sharp. One of the first solid foods he ate was sugar-coated cereal, which he loved. But we let him have only small amounts of it.

Ceecee was fond of all of us, but Jamie was his favorite and even after he grew up, he went on talking "baby talk" to her as a little raccoon talks to its mother and as the mother talks to him. The sound is a kind of deep *"ptrrrr . . . ptrrrr . . . ptrrrr."* When Jamie called to him, he would answer with a high, whimpering whine.

During the warm weather Jamie took him out in the garden and let him climb an oak tree. After he had climbed to a high place, he would settle down in a fork that seemed comfortable and doze and swing all afternoon. In the early evening he came down again and went to the patio door for his supper. He was eating only four meals a day now, breakfast, lunch, supper, and at bedtime.

One day when he was starting up the tree trunk, he slipped and fell. It gave him quite a jolt and he seemed to think he had been hurt. Sitting on the ground, he began to feel his body with both hands, patting his back, his stomach, his chest, arms, and legs, as though he thought, I *must* have a broken bone *someplace!* Jamie laughed.

Soon after he was weaned, Ceecee would watch us go into   63

the dining room at mealtime and sit down at the table to eat. He decided he belonged there, too. After that, when I called Lee and Jamie to dinner, he would come, too, climbing up on the fourth chair and sitting with his little hands folded, as if waiting to be served. I would bring him a small plate of sugar-coated cereal and he would eat the grains politely, one at a time, picking them up in his little fingers.

Raccoons sometimes wash and soften their food before eating it, but not always. We kept a large, heavy flowerpot saucer of water for Ceecee, and when he began to eat pieces of chicken or fruit, he would usually wash them there. Like all raccoons, he never watched what he was doing, but stared up at the ceiling all the time he was dabbling and scrubbing in the water.

Before long we found that he could eat only certain foods

and for a good reason. He had been injured internally by his fall in the chimney and would never be able to eat as other raccoons eat or take care of himself in the wild. We had planned to release him in the spring, but now we knew we would have to keep him and take care of him. But we didn't mind, though we were sorry he could never have a free life.

One cloudy fall day he went out of doors and climbed up the oak tree as usual. While he was there a storm came up, and soon a cloudburst broke. Rain came down in sheets and wind lashed the branches of the trees. All of a sudden a scared and soaking-wet little coon appeared at the patio door, calling for Jamie. He had never seen rain before or felt a harsh wind. Now he looked terrified and he could scarcely wait for the door to be opened. As if he felt like saying, "Come quick, Mommy! Something terrible has happened!" Jamie said.

Lee built a "den" for him about the size of a large log and put it at one end of the sun porch. Here, curled up on a blanket, he slept most of the day, snoring almost as loud as Sugar, the little groundhog, had snored. (And a groundhog can snore louder than the biggest man.) Now and then he came out to get a drink of water, to climb up and rock in the rocking chair, which he loved, or to get into some sort of mischief.

About that time we had a little fox squirrel which had been brought to me because he had a broken leg. He was so ragged and dirty that I named him Ragamuffin, but we called him Muff.

His leg had healed nicely but he was still weak and thin and not yet ready to go back to the wild. He, too, lived on the sun porch in a small cage of his own, sleeping in a blanket-filled box. Muff was so glad to be warm, fed, and comfortable that being in the cage didn't bother him at all. Here he played, ate,

65

drank, and slept and just wanted to be left alone. But Ceecee kept teasing him. He seized Muff's cage and shook it, rattling the door and doing other things to annoy him.

One evening I heard an angry squall from Muff and rushed out to see what was going on, only to find that Ceecee had worked his busy little hand through the wires of Muff's cage and was stealing and eating Muff's walnuts. Ceecee was nocturnal and woke up about the time Muff went to sleep, for most squirrels go to sleep around dusk. Sometimes he would tease and wake Muff by pushing the squirrel cage around the floor with a crashing banging sound. This was not hard for him to do, as raccoons are strong for their size. Or he would slip up and pull Muff's tail while Muff was asleep, with a pleased look on his face something like an evil grin.

One night when he reached into the cage to steal a walnut, Muff woke up, shot out of his box, and bit Ceecee's hand hard enough to make it bleed. Ceecee went around shaking and licking his hand, and he never again tried to steal the walnuts—unless he was sure that Muff was covered up and really asleep.

Ceecee slept most of the day, first in his basket or cage or in the oak tree, later in the "den" Lee built for him. He would wake up around sunset, eat his supper, and stay up until about ten P.M. Then he would wake up about midnight and be up the rest of the night.

When he was a baby, whoever gave him his last bottle would sit down in the sun-porch rocking chair to feed him. He was used to this and even after he grew up, he wanted to be rocked before he went back to bed for his ten o'clock nap. He would come to the room where we were sitting and make a complaining, burbling sound. We knew what he wanted and would start asking, "Who's going to rock the coon tonight?" We took turns

at this, but he seemed happiest to have Jamie do it. Often he would go to her closed door and lie down and wait faithfully for her to come out.

In the woods raccoons spend their nights hunting and fishing for food and drinking at streams, sometimes traveling in pairs. Their little hands are busy all the time and they will often treat stones, sticks, nutshells, and other objects like toys, turning them over and over, rolling them around, washing them and playing with them. And on moonlit nights raccoons may spend a lot of time sitting in the doors of their tree-trunk dens, just looking around. For some reason the moon seems to interest them very much, especially when it is round and full.

On many a moonlit night I have seen Ceecee rocking slowly, looking out at the moon, his eyes like yellow jewels in the dark. In many states it is against the law for men known as coon hunters to use these glowing eyes as targets. But there are always some who have no respect for law or for fairness.

NIBBY, THE COTTONTAIL RABBIT

The first baby rabbit I ever had was named Nibbles because nibbling seemed to be his favorite occupation. Since then I have had other baby rabbits, I am sorry to say. Sorry because they should have been left where they were found, to grow up in the care of their mothers, since they were not really lost or orphaned.

One day there was a knock at the door and I opened it to find a little boy and girl standing there. The boy had a covered basket.

"We found a baby rabbit this afternoon," he said, "and he didn't have any mother. So we thought maybe you'd take care of him."

I asked, "Where did you find him?"

He said, "We went on a picnic in the state park, and us kids were looking for Indian relics and stuff, and all of a sudden I saw this baby rabbit sitting there all by itself. Lost. So we thought we'd better bring it to you because if it hasn't got any mother, something might hurt it . . . or eat it."

This has happened many times. Each time I have tried to explain that just because we see a baby rabbit alone, we should not assume that he has no mother. Sometimes I can take the baby

69

back to the nest and leave it there, but with Nibby this was impossible. The state park was miles away and the children couldn't remember just where they had picked him up, though it must have been near his nest.

The nest which a mother rabbit prepares for her babies is about three inches deep, about five inches across, and six or seven inches long. She scratches it out in a spot that seems safe and dry, often in a garden, lawn, meadow, or at the edge of a woods. She then lines it with soft grass and with fur which she pulls from her own breast.

Here the babies sleep peacefully (unless some intruder disturbs them) until they are old enough to get out and play. The mother feeds them around daylight, again at dusk, and in the night. The rest of the time she is away from the nest, foraging for her own food or sleeping through the daylight hours. They grow fast and at three weeks can get out of the nest and scamper around, hopping, jumping, and playing, but return to the nest to meet their mother at feeding time. Now and then some person sees one of them trying to hide in the grass and thinks he is lost or has been deserted or that his mother has been killed. To pick him up and take him away is kindly meant, but it is not really kind, for most of the babies carried from their natural homes soon die.

Nibby was a very young rabbit. His eyes were open, but he was still tiny, covered with soft gray hair. Being carried around had not been good for him, and he was hungry and chilled. I put him in a warm pet blanket, laid him in a deep box, and covered it with a small screen held firmly in place by a heavy book.

This might seem unnecessary, but baby rabbits can jump quite high, even at an early age, and can get through very small spaces. Unless their box or basket is well covered, they are likely to jump out, fall and hurt themselves, and lie there unnoticed until they die of injury or exposure.

I gave Nibby his formula with a medicine dropper, but began using the pet bottle as soon as he was able to take it, about a week. I fed him on the same schedule his mother would have used—about four times a day—and was extremely careful not to overfeed him. He grew very fast and his hair became thicker and browner. By the time he was two weeks old (I think) he was beginning to nibble, so I started him on solid food. Later he was especially pleased with the greens I gathered for him and ate them as fast as possible, his nose twitching all the time.

Nibby was an eastern cottontail. As he grew older, his coat became browner, his tail was brown on top, but when he ran it turned up and looked exactly like a ball of cotton.

A baby cottontail weighs only an ounce when it is born, and its eyes are closed. It is naked until its first gray hairs begin to grow, but it has teeth, even though they are barely through the gums. The mother takes good care of the babies, and if she thinks they are in danger, she will move them one by one to a new nest, carrying them in her mouth. She does her best to protect them from enemies, such as dogs, cats, foxes, crows, owls, hawks, and other enemies, including man. (I once saw a mother rabbit leap three feet high, again and again, to fight off a crow that was trying to take her little ones.)

By the time Nibby was about a month old he had a full set of teeth, something to remember. A rabbit's teeth are sharp, and anyone who handles him carelessly may be bitten.

Nibby liked being handled and petted. Some cottontails do not like to be handled, however, and never become tame. I liked to watch him wash his face, scrubbing it with his paws, then   71

scrubbing his ears and smoothing his coat. Rabbits make few sounds that we can hear, but he squealed sometimes when he was hungry and thumped the floor with his big hind foot the way rabbits thump the ground.

In the wild grown-up rabbits spend most of their time in forms. A form is a resting place in thick grass, under a brush heap, or in a thicket. They like to sit in the sun, too, especially on winter days. If the weather is extremely cold or the snow is deep, they may seek shelter in a woods or hole up in the burrow of a groundhog.

They may also use a groundhog hole as a place to hide from their enemies. Or they may "freeze" in deep grass and remain there without moving, for fifteen to twenty minutes, if a hunter or some other enemy is near. Though they usually hop along quite slowly, they can run very fast when they wish and, when pursued by an enemy, can make a single leap as long as fifteen feet.

As soon as Nibby was old enough (about six weeks), we took him out into our garden and released him in a thick hedge-row where we have planted a large amount of cover for birds and animals.

Evidently he liked his new home, for he is still living there. Rabbits like to feed around dusk, and on many late afternoons I have seen Nibby hopping slowly around the garden, stretching up "on tiptoe" to eat grass seed or berries from tasty plants. At daylight I have watched him feeding on crab apples fallen from the tree by our patio and have seen him in the moonlight feasting on birdseed at our ground feeder.

Whether or not Nibby "remembers" me I do not know, but he seems to understand that I am not to be feared and does not run away when I am near. He is now two years old, and since cottontail rabbits often live five years in captivity, Nibby will probably live just as long in our protected garden.

Last year he found a mate in this woodsy neighborhood. And now we not only have Nibby and his mate to watch but a pair of twins as well.

DITTY, THE FOX SQUIRREL

I think there are no animals more interesting, playful, or lovable than fox squirrels. We have befriended and brought up nearly twenty of them over the years, and they often gave us the feeling that they were not squirrels at all, but small furry elves.

All of these squirrels were orphans that had been found and rescued after their mothers were killed:

Groany, the fussiest	Deedee, the sweetest
Mimi, the prettiest	Francie, the wildest
Shad, the gentlest	Gabby, the talkingest
Willie, the shyest	Dandy, the handsomest
Chip, the smartest	Muff, first called Ragamuffin
Louie, the sassiest	Star, named for her pretty white mark
Jemmy, the smallest	Brother and Sister, furry twins
Jimmy, the weakest	Richard, named for Dr. Siebert

And *Ditty,* who seemed so stupid.

Nearly all of them were past six weeks old when they came to us and most of them had their eyes open. Their little ears were standing up and covered with fur, though the ears of a newborn baby lie flat against its head.

Our first squirrel foundlings were a litter of three, rescued after their mother was killed by a truck. But since then we have never had more than two at one time and usually only one. We fed them as explained on page 132, first with a medicine dropper and then with a Pet Nip nursing bottle (see page 89). A squirrel with a nursing bottle is a very appealing sight, as he soon learns to hold it in his hands and sometimes in both hands and feet.

Little squirrels love attention and will purr like kittens when stroked or petted. If two or more are kept in the same box or basket, they will sleep snuggled against each other.

As they are growing up, they spend a lot of time talking together with a *cr-rrrrronk . . . cr-rrrrronk* sound. This is a form of "baby talk" and they never use it after they are grown. Our first babies were very loving and would climb up on our knees and "talk" to us with friendly little *mm . . . mm . . . mm* sounds and ride around on our shoulders. Groany, my first fox squirrel, would come running to meet me in the mornings, throw his furry little arms around my ankle, and refuse to let go even when I was walking around the kitchen making the coffee. When I took forbidden objects away from him, he squalled angrily at times. At other times he just complained with a low, grumbling sound.

No woods animal is more playful. Like acrobats, squirrels leap, jump, twist, spin, run, hop, roll, and bounce, alone or with others. They will chase one another around and around, roll and wrestle and tumble on the floor.

Wild squirrels are often seen playing hide-and-seek on the trunk of a tree. One will vanish on the back and cling there, hiding quietly. The other hunts for him, and the moment he finds him they are off again, racing around the tree, giving you the feeling that they are laughing merrily.

Even tiny fox squirrels will bark at strangers or strange

noises and at all bluejays, for these birds seem to be their natural enemies. All squirrels will chatter when they are displeased about something. Our sassy little Mimi used to chatter at me and scold me angrily when I took a forbidden object away from her.

They wash as a kitten washes, with much scrubbing of arms, head, chest, and face. Then they dry with their tails. A squirrel's tail is very important to him. It helps him to balance when he leaps from branch to branch and acts as a "parachute" to protect him from hard falls. It shields him from rain, heat, and cold. It is his umbrella and his towel. He puffs it up and makes it large and scary when he wants to frighten away a stranger or an enemy. It even shields him from his enemies . . . or at least he seems to think so. For when he sees any strange object which just might *be* an enemy, he walks past it cautiously, spreading his tail in such a way that it screens him from view. Apparently he believes that if he can't see *it*, it can't see *him*.

A fox squirrel uses his tail for "talking" in a sign language understood by all squirrels and by some birds and other animals. We learned to understand it very well. A playful flip of the tip means, "Come on! Let's play!" A sudden flounce, especially when the squirrel is drowsy, means, "Oh, go away!" When he is startled or perhaps afraid, he jerks his tail back and forth, barking and chattering at the same time. When he is really angry, his tail goes around and around.

All fox squirrels have temper tantrums and we could not help laughing at them. When Chip was angry, he barked and chattered at the top of his voice. His tail jerked around and around, his whiskers bristled, his nose twitched, he made short lunges with his front feet while stamping his back feet. Gabby, though a very appealing animal, had a short temper and frequent tantrums. Like all squirrels, he was much stronger than most people would believe and could do surprising things. Once, while we cleaned his sleeping cage, we put him in a birdcage to keep him out of mischief. This made him so furious that he tore the birdcage to pieces. He and all the others performed feats of strength astonishing to us. We have seen a fox squirrel pick up a hammer in his mouth and walk away with it. Another seized a whole large ear of corn in his teeth and leaped 'through the trees with it.

Many people seem to think that squirrels eat only nuts and corn, but these animals like and hunt for many other foods. (See list on page 134.) They need the hard shells of nuts such as black walnuts to keep their teeth ground short. If a squirrel's teeth become too long and he has no way to grind them down, they will turn back into his mouth and even grow into the roof of his mouth. He will not be able to eat and will starve to death. In the wild this may happen not only to squirrels but to any other gnawing animal, such as groundhogs, chipmunks, raccoons.

Many people have the mistaken idea that a squirrel belongs to the rat family simply because both are rodents.

This word comes from the Latin *rodere*, which means "to gnaw." Therefore, *all* gnawing animals are rodents. A rat is a rodent, but all rodents are not rats.

Rodents include beavers, tree squirrels, chipmunks, marmots, porcupines, groundhogs, prairie dogs, gophers, groundsquirrels, flying squirrels, muskrats, white-footed mice, and many others. Rabbits are not true rodents, but are considered rodent-like.

Squirrels need a good deal of water and often lick dew from plants and grasses. They drink from birdbaths, puddles, and little pools or creeks. In winter they sometimes eat snow. A fox squirrel who finds a birdbath full of frozen water will sit on it or lie down on it until some of the ice melts to form drinking water. All our animals drank the water we put in their cages except Groany. He would climb up to the kitchen sink and drink from the water tap when it was turned on for him in a thin stream.

Animals differ as much as humans in appearance, coloring, personality, and habits, and no two are exactly alike. Groany was a dandy, always brushing his coat and combing his tail with his teeth and claws. Mimi acted as though she hated to bathe and never gave herself more than "a lick and a promise" in the mornings.

Chip was the smartest fox squirrel I have ever known. He understood that knobs have something to do with opening doors. When he wanted to go into the next room and found the door closed, he would climb up on a nearby chair and rattle the knob with his little hands. He was very loving toward Jamie and would always "kiss" her when she fed him, putting his mouth softly against her cheek.

Deedee was delicate, Willie was shy and quiet, Dandy was bold, curious, and unafraid. Francie was wild and untamed. Even as a very small squirrel she would pace her cage like a restless tiger. She showed no interest in any of us and, unlike the others, didn't want us to hold her or pet her. The day we gave her her freedom she ran up a locust tree, a bright streak of fur, swung through the branches as easily as Tarzan, and never missed a leap . . . or us. She did not even look back. She was the only animal we sheltered that cared nothing for love from us. She was truly of the wild.

Some animals have formed close friendships. Richard and Deedee played together as babies. When we released them they
set up housekeeping in the big maple and had children of their

own. But Richard was very fond of me and never forgot me. He still came when I called him, would "visit" at the patio door, or peer in at me through the window.

Brother and Sister grew up together and were always gentle and affectionate toward each other. Even after they were grown, they sometimes ate together, which is very unusual, as adult squirrels do not like to share their meals. When we released them in the garden, they built a nest together and Sister, at least, was content there. But Brother often followed at my heels when I went outside, and I think he always liked the sun porch better than the garden.

Little Jemmy lived on the sun porch when we had Susie Possum and took a great interest in watching her pace up and down. Each of them had a sleeping box on the floor, but one chilly morning when I went in to feed them, Jemmy had disappeared. Here was a mystery, for the windows were closed, the patio door locked, and the door that opened into the rest of the house had been closed all night. There was no way Jemmy could get out . . . but he was gone, just the same.

I hunted for ten or fifteen minutes before I found him. I searched everything in sight. I found that he had grown chilly toward morning, when the weather changed, and after Susie Possum went to sleep, he climbed into bed with her and snuggled up to her for warmth. Susie never knew she had a roommate (or boxmate) and did not even wake up when I took him out and tucked him into warm blankets of his own.

One day a boy brought me a baby squirrel he had found under a tree after the mother had been killed by a car. We had already raised thirteen baby fox squirrels, so I named this one Louie the Fourteenth. Louie was never a very affectionate squirrel, but I think he liked me, and I know he never forgot me.

79

Even after he grew up and had a home in our garden, he came back for visits. Every morning he would scratch on the patio door like a puppy until I opened it. Then he would bounce in, eat a good breakfast, and bounce out again.

Watching these animals, I found that squirrels learn from one another, even imitate one another, as do many animals and birds.

In his babyhood Chip had been shot out of a tree by the hunter who killed his mother. Whether or not this was the reason, I do not know, but he was afraid of falling and would never jump like other squirrels. Then came Gabby, who was a very daring jumper. Gabby would leap from my shoulder to the sofa and then from the sofa back to my shoulder. Gabby and I played jump for an hour at a time, with Chip watching from a distance.

Chip was always jealous of Gabby and often tried to chase him away. And after a while, though plainly uncertain and still afraid, Chip began to jump. He would climb to the top of his sleeping cage and then jump to my shoulder or into Jamie's arms. As time passed, he jumped more and more often and finally seemed to get over his fear.

In spite of his sharp temper, Chip was a friendly little fellow. He would go from Jamie to Lee and then to me, waiting for his head to be petted. One day Gabby started doing the same thing.

When Chip wanted his breakfast, he would seize the door of his sleeping cage and shake it until it rattled. Gabby learned this, and they would both shake their doors at once, making a dreadful racket, until I fed them.

Muffin, who lived on the sun porch when we had Ceecee the raccoon, spent a lot of time watching him wash food in a flat clay saucer of water. Later Muffin began going to this same saucer to wash a nut. Ceecee liked nuts, too, but never buried one in a blanket like a squirrel until he saw Muff do it.

All our animals seemed so smart that I was surprised to find one that wasn't. Ditty.

Ditty and Star were sisters, whose mother was killed on a country road. They were beautiful little animals, just about old enough to venture out of the nest. We gave Star her name because of the white mark under her chin.

Ditty was sweet and pretty and had the shiniest black eyes I had ever seen. But she seemed stupid.

Star seized her small nursing bottle and held it with both hands while she drank from it. Ditty dropped hers on the floor. Star climbed out of their basket, skipped across the room and back again. Ditty climbed out and got lost. Star saw a bluejay at the window and barked at him. Ditty stared at her as if she wondered what all the fuss was about and didn't even notice him.

These little sisters came to us in late spring and by late summer they were old enough to be released. Star, though lively, was a very ordinary-looking squirrel except for the white mark. But Ditty was colorful, with a fluffy tail, a cream-colored stomach, big eyes, and a rich reddish-brown coat. We released them in the garden in plenty of time for them to find a new home before fall and get it ready for winter.

Squirrels usually live in warm dens in the winter and in cool nests in the summer. They like to den in dead trees if they can, for a living tree keeps on growing, and after a while the entrance will start closing up. Of course they can keep gnawing it open, but that is a lot of gnawing. We did not have any dead trees, but there were some that had been damaged by storms. Holes were left where the limbs had been torn off. These holes make fine nesting places for squirrels, also for owls and other birds, such as woodpeckers.

A squirrel's den inside a tree is always two or three feet down, too far to be reached by the busy hands of a nosy raccoon. The mother carries in various kinds of nesting materials—leaves, grasses, mint, milkweed, cornhusks, moss, even paper tissues—whatever she can find that is suitable. Here nuts are stored and baby squirrels are born.

If all the nesting holes are taken, however, or if the weather is very hot, a squirrel will build a special outdoor nest, usually in the fork of a tree or on a strong branch. It is quite large, with a sturdy frame of twigs, walls made of many layers of leaves to keep out the weather, even a ceiling also of leaves. The small owner goes in and out through a hallway at one side.

When we left Star and Ditty in the garden, we left food for them, too, fruit and nuts on a feeding shelf. Both ran up a large tree and looked around. Star swung from branch to branch and then leaped easily into another tree.

Ditty, too, began swinging through the branches. Then she made a leap—the worst I ever saw. She barely reached the next tree, where she clung to a twig, kicking and struggling to keep from falling, lucky to have reached it at all.

The weather was still warm and pleasant and each of them started to build a summer nest. Star built a beautiful nest in the fork of an oak tree, cool and leafy and weathertight. The nest Ditty built wouldn't even stay together. It collapsed before it was half finished, and most of it fell down on the ground.

Both Star and Ditty came to the feeding shelf to look for goodies. Star took a nut, ran over to a small log, and sat there while she ate it. Ditty took a nut, ran to another small log, and fell off it.

Soon afterward there was a summer storm followed by three days of drenching rain. I was worried about the squirrels, since the out-of-doors was new to them, but felt sure Star was all right. I saw her running to the feeding shelf for food, going in and out of her nice new house. I did not see Ditty at all.

The next day Lori, a little girl down the street, found a small fox squirrel lying under a tree. It did not run when she stooped down to look at it, and because it seemed so tame, she tried to pick it up and it bit her. It was Ditty.

When any person in our town is bitten by a strange animal, the animal (if it can be found) must be kept in a cage or some other sort of shelter for twenty-one days. During this time it is closely watched by a veterinarian to see if it has rabies, a dreadful disease for which there's no cure. But no animal can just "catch" or "take" rabies. He must be bitten by another animal to get it, one that is already sick.

In our part of the country very few animals (except skunks and bats) have rabies. If an animal *is* infected with it, he will

83

soon die, which is why he is closely watched. If he is well and lively at the end of twenty-one days, it is assumed that he does not have rabies and that the person he bit is out of danger. If he does die, treatment is started at once. The person who has been bitten by an infected animal must take some very painful shots, unless he has already been vaccinated for the disease, which most people have not.

That is why it is dangerous (and very foolish) to try to feed a wild squirrel by hand. To a squirrel anything hard is a nut, and he may mistake your fingernail for one. If he bites you and then scampers away, you cannot know whether he is sick or well, and to be on the safe side, you may have to take the painful shots.

When we called to report that a little girl had been bitten, a man from the Health Department came to get Ditty. He thought she might be sick because she had made no effort to run up the tree, but I thought she was in shock. All squirrels are sensitive animals and can easily go into shock when they are handled by strangers. This means that they "freeze" with fear, lose consciousness, and sometimes die. Ditty was limp and quiet, scarcely breathing, and her eyes were glazed. We brought her small sleeping cage and gently lifted her into it.

I did not think she could have rabies, but she had to be confined and watched, to make sure. The man from the Health Department decided she should spend her twenty-one days of confinement with me, since I knew how to care for her. During this time Dr. Siebert would come regularly to examine her.

Ditty was almost dead when I got her home. Gently, I began giving her water, putting it into her mouth with a medicine dropper. I had not seen her since before the storm and felt sure she must have been lying under that tree for three days, injured, and with no food at all.

Dr. Siebert came to check her. She was not ill, he said, but she had broken both her arms. When he told me this, I remembered her first clumsy leap. No doubt she had made another leap like that, missed the branch, and fallen.

I gave her *half* a baby aspirin (the orange flavor she liked), crushing it in a teaspoon until it was powder, then adding a little water and putting it into her mouth with the dropper. It eased her pain and kept her quiet. When she had had more water and a little food, I covered her warmly and she went to sleep. Being at home with me helped her a great deal, for squirrels and other sensitive animals may die in unfamiliar surroundings.

When she woke up she was hungry and I gave her a small meal, feeding her by hand. Then she drank a little more water and her eyes cleared. I felt sure she would get well.

Slowly her arms healed. Since a squirrel will not tolerate a splint or bandage, we could help her only by keeping her quiet, sleepy, and content. At the end of twenty-one days she was well and strong, and both she and Lori were out of danger.

I looked at Ditty as she played around the sun porch, wondering what to do with her. Poor little thing, I thought. She couldn't even leap from one branch to another, sit on a stump, or find her way home!

The last time Dr. Siebert came to see her he said, "She's all right now . . . except for one thing. She was born with defective eyesight and sees very poorly. I'm afraid she can never take care of herself in the wild. She could easily come to harm. You'll probably have to keep her."

"Well," I said, "we won't mind." I picked her up and stroked her gently. Poor little Ditty. She wasn't stupid, after all. She was partly blind.

CARE AND INSTRUCTION

GENERAL CARE FOR SMALL WILD ANIMALS

IMMEDIATE EMERGENCY CARE

First of all, even before food and water, the baby animal must have rest, warmth, and quiet.

Put it in a safe and comfortable place and cover it. Give it time to feel safe, at least half an hour, without noise and confusion around it. Do not let people rush in to look at it, and do not let anyone handle it. It should be handled only by the person or persons who will be caring for it reguarly.

Items needed. *A box or basket* of a size to be comfortable for the animal. It should not be too large, or the baby will be cold. It must not be too small, however, or the baby will be crowded and hot. Line it with paper; then use animal blankets or the animal cradle described below.

Animal blankets. These are squares of soft, old terry towels which have been torn up. They can be of various sizes.

Animal cradle. This is a terry-cloth toilet-seat cover turned upside down and drawn up to make a nest. Line it with several layers of soft paper, such as facial tissue.

88

Nursing bottle. You can buy these at pet stores or from a veterinarian. One of the best is called a NIP Pet Nurser. It is made just like a human baby's bottle, only smaller, and comes with a tiny brush and extra nipples. To make a hole in one of these nipples, puncture it with a red-hot needle which has been heated in the flame of a match. The hole should be a size to allow the milk to flow comfortably, but not too fast. (Milk which flows too fast will come frothing out the baby animal's nose.) *Do not* try to use doll bottles. In an emergency a human baby bottle can be used, but it is often awkward and uncomfortable for tiny babies, though it can be used successfully when they are older.

Heating pad or hot water bottle.

Medicine dropper (preferably plastic) and a *pipe cleaner* for cleaning it.

A *cover*, well ventilated, for the box or basket. This is important, as even a small baby may get out and die of exposure. Sometimes a cake cooling rack can be used to cover the box, with a heavy book on top to keep it in place. A small window screen is much safer. A heavy book can be used on this, too. However, you will not need a cover for a box or basket kept in a cage.

Directions for using above items. Put the baby in the box or basket, which you have prepared as explained in items above. Do not use shavings or "kitty litter" material in it, as the dust from these may harm the animal. Line his bed with facial tissue or paper towels rather than with newspaper, as the printing ink may be harmful, though it is all right to use newspapers on the floor of a cage. Cover the baby with several animal blankets. He will not smother. Do not fold them, but have them loose and airy.

If the weather is cold and the baby seems chilly (foundlings 89 often are) use a hot-water bottle or heating pad to warm the box, but *DO NOT put it in with the animal.* If a hot-water bottle is used, it should be only moderately warm and moderately full. *Refill it regularly.* Use as directed for a heating pad.

A heating pad is best because you do not have to remember to refill it. But do not set the box directly on top of it because it is as harmful for the baby to be too hot as to be too cold. Place two or three magazines, folded newspapers, or thick folded towels between the box and the pad. Test the bed with your hand. It should be just warm, never hot. If it seems too warm, add more papers or towels.

If you own a fairly large cage or can get one, set the box or basket in this to keep the baby from being molested by other pet animals or curious visitors. Place the heat under the cage.

IMMEDIATE FEEDINGS

Emergency formula. Most tiny orphan animals are in a state of shock when they are found and should be given a formula which will help to relieve the dehydration and blood-sugar loss which accompanies this condition.

Dr. Robert L. Stevensons, of Dayton, Ohio, who has saved many animal babies, uses this emergency formula:

> ¾ cup of distilled warm water
> 1 level teaspoon of powdered skim milk
> ¼ teaspoon of strained honey
>
> Mix thoroughly.

For tiny babies only a few days old:
Feed 2–5 drops with an eyedropper every 2–4 hours.

The amount may be increased proportionately with the size of the animal.

This formula is given the first 24 hours and may be used longer if necessary. If the baby animal seems to be doing well, however, the regular milk formula may be started after 24 hours have passed.

Milk formula. (See possum care and raccoon care chapters for variations to be used.)

> 1 cup of whole milk (scalded* but *not* boiled)
> 1 level tablespoon of white Karo syrup
> *Scalded means heating to just before boiling.

GENERAL FEEDING INSTRUCTIONS

Food. Feeding directions followed after emergency care has been given are described separately in individual sections for the baby animals.

For the milk formula use whole milk (unless otherwise directed) and *be sure* to scald it; do not let it boil even a little. Cool it to lukewarm. (We have also used Enfamil, a ready-mixed baby formula, with good results.)

Any unused formula should be kept covered in the refrigerator. When you wish to heat it, put what you will need in the nursing bottle, using a small funnel. Then warm the bottle under hot, running water or set it in a bowl of hot water for a little while. Test a few drops on your wrist, as for a baby. If it is too hot, run cold water over it for a second or two and test again.

Have the food fresh and sweet, and clean the bottle and nipple thoroughly after every feeding.

If necessary, feedings for a tiny animal can be started with a medicine dropper. Clean the dropper with a pipe cleaner immediately after using it, and keep the plastic part in cold water until it is needed again.

Feed slowly, and do not overfeed, or the baby will die. (See individual chapters on each animal for amounts.) Very tiny babies are usually started on 4 or 5 drops of formula (less than half a medicine dropper), especially if they have been without food for some time. This can be increased to 1 teaspoonful and then to the amount given in the chapter about that particular animal.

Feeding blanket. The baby will feel safer and it will be easier for you to handle him if you wrap him lightly and hold him lightly when you feed him, firmly but not too tightly. A soft terry washcloth or a small terry animal blanket will be fine.

Preparing bottles. Never put more formula in a bottle than you intend to use at one feeding. If you do, the animal may drink more than he should before you realize it and can easily die from such overfeeding.

WEANING

Weaning (giving up milk for solid food) is always started soon after the baby's eyes are open, not before, with a cereal formula (see page 146). The time for weaning varies with the animal. Some young animals simply refuse their milk when they are ready for solid food. Others keep taking the formula, but develop diarrhea, which (after their eyes are open) is an indication that they should be weaned. The transition to solid food is easy and safe if directions are followed carefully.

VITAMINS

Do not give vitamins to tiny babies.

When older animals *show a need* for them (see page 23), Zyma Drops, often used for human babies, or Pet Drops, a similar solution for animals, may be used. Some animals reject them, however, because of the strong cod-liver-oil smell. You can disguise this by adding the vitamins to nut balls (see page 146) or by placing a tiny bit of the vitamin liquid on food such as nut pieces, apple slivers, etc., and exposing these to the air until the odor is somewhat dissipated. Use only 3 or 4 drops to a full nut ball recipe. Never give an animal more than is shown by the first mark on the dropper.

HANDLING THE BABY

Never forcibly restrain an animal unless this is absolutely necessary, and then only momentarily. Such restraint is very frightening to him and could cause him to go into shock and die. Sometimes, when you are ready to take a small animal out of his cage for a feeding, he will panic and cling to the wire or to the edge of his box. *Never try to force him to let go*, as such pulling might break his tender bones. Soothe him, let him relax, and then very gently pry him loose.

If he should get out of his cage, don't panic and don't start chasing him because this will terrify and exhaust him. If food and water are left in his cage and the door is left open, he will usually go back into it after a while, especially when things are quiet. Even if he hides somewhere and stays away for several hours, be patient. He might even stay away until after dark, but he will return when he is hungry.

If the room is so cold that he could become chilled, or if he is likely to come to harm in some way, such as gnawing an electric wire, you may have to catch him.

The easiest way is to throw a large, soft towel over him. When covered, he will probably feel safe and remain quiet. You can then pick him up by grasping him, gently but firmly, through

93

the towel. Sometimes a net can be used successfully, but if the little animal becomes tangled in it, he may hurt himself or suffer shock or panic. (And a small animal can die very quickly from shock.) We use a net only as a last resort and then gently.

Warnings. *Never* seize an animal by the tail. Lift him gently but firmly, by holding him across his back, at the shoulders, with one hand and supporting his chest with the other hand.

Do not drop him because he kicks, which is a natural reaction, and do not be alarmed by any noise he may make, such as squalling, as this, too, is normal.

If you seize a squirrel's tail, most of it will come off and never grow back. In an emergency you can seize him where the tail joins the body, but do not seize the tail itself.)

Sometimes when an animal is allowed to play outside its cage, he may find and put into his mouth some object he should not have. Instead of trying to take the object away from him (which you probably couldn't do anyway), offer a substitute. He will usually drop the first object to take the second, especially if the second is some sort of treat.

VERMIN

Sometimes a baby animal is infested with wood lice (black, white, or red mites) or, worse still, maggots. These are very unpleasant, of course, but you must deal with them if you really want to help the animal. *Never use commercial insecticides*. They are poisonous to all animals.

For lice. Buy a box of chamomile tea at a drugstore or health food store. Make it according to the directions on the box and let it steep, or soak, until it is fairly strong. This tea is a safe repellent. Dampen a Q-Tip or tissue in the tea and lightly smooth it through the animal's fur without getting it really wet. This will usually eliminate the wood lice. It is often possible to remove them with your fingers, too.

For maggots. These look like large, fat grains of rice which are constantly moving or twisting. They are usually found in wounds, sometimes in the animal's eyes. I have always removed them from wounds with eyebrow tweezers, working quickly but carefully. Then flush the wound with chamomile tea, peroxide, or Bactine. The suction of an empty medicine dropper will remove small maggots from a baby's eyes or lift out large ones, but be careful. Flush the eyes with chamomile tea, which will not harm them, or with cooled, boiled water. Do not use anything else in the eyes. Watch daily to see if more maggots hatch out. If so, destroy them in the same way.

ILLNESS

Diarrhea in small babies. Decrease the white Karo in a feeding and wait to see if this helps the situation.

If the animal has diarrhea, add 2 or 3 drops of Kaopectate to a feeding. (I had to do this for a baby squirrel that had been given egg in its formula, which is wrong.)

Constipation. This happens so rarely it is hardly necessary to mention. Be sure the condition really exists before you attempt to treat it. Increasing the Karo in a feeding by a few drops will usually correct it. Experiment to find the right formula.

If the condition should persist, add 2 or 3 drops of fresh mineral oil to a feeding. But don't be in a hurry to do this!

Safety measure. Furry animals often develop a serious, even fatal liver trouble.

An old-time remedy is 1 or 2 drops of white vinegar in the drinking water each day. While I have no proof that this prevents the ailment, many persons from rural areas say they have used the plan successfully, even for dogs, and it is harmless.

FASTENING A CAGE

Latches which may seem secure can often be opened by the small, clever fingers of raccoons, groundhogs, or squirrels. When we found our latches inadequate, we tried many other ways of securing the cages, including snap clothespins, twists of wire, etc. The only fastener the animals could not open was a "dog snap" of sturdy construction, the kind used to fasten a leash to a collar. We used two or three of these on each cage door.

FOOD WARNINGS

Be careful never to give any animal bark, fruit, or leaves unless you know what you are doing. Among poisonous items are cherry twigs, certain locust blooms, and many leaves including peach leaves.

Clover, rose petals, dandelion leaves, and the like should always be carefully washed since they may have been sprayed with some harmful chemical.

No matter *who* recommends it, never give egg yolk to baby squirrels; they cannot tolerate it and will die.

Do not give an animal cheese or anything moldy, since these can cause death also.

BATHING

Always keep clean, fresh water before your animal.

No animal should ever be bathed with detergent or shampoo since these will dry its skin and cause it to become sore and itchy. Use *only* a mild soap or a baby shampoo of pure soap.

TEETH

All gnawing animals must keep their teeth ground down. If the teeth become too long, the animals suffer great pain, cannot eat, and will starve to death. Give the appropriate gnawing materials to each animal:

Groundhog. English walnuts, preferably unshelled
Squirrel. Slightly cracked walnuts, hickory nuts, or pecans, unshelled
Possum. English walnuts, beechnuts, pecans, all uncracked
Chickaree. Hard toast, zwieback, hard-shell nuts
Raccoon. English walnuts, pecans, uncracked
Rabbit. Stout twigs, preferably apple twigs. (Squirrels like these, too.)

PROTECTING AGAINST DISEASE

People often ask, "Are there any diseases which I can get from animals?"

The answer is yes . . . and there are also diseases which you can get from people, your family, friends, or neighbors. So guarding against pet diseases isn't too different from guarding against human diseases.

You will probably be working with baby animals only, as older animals cannot be tamed and should not be handled except for treatment by a veterinarian, in rescue, or for convalescent care.

In handling a baby animal, especially a new and unfamiliar one, do not place it on a table or any other surface used by hu-   97 mans for eating or preparing food. Any surface should be covered with thick newspapers.

After handling the animal, wash your hands thoroughly, *not* at the kitchen sink or where food is prepared, but in a bathroom or basement basin.

Wash bedding or animal blankets separately, with a very small amount of bleach in the wash water. Do not wash bedding or blankets with the family laundry. Rinse well.

Newspapers used in cages or for waste should be rolled up and burned or tied into a plastic or paper bag for disposal and put outside in trash containers.

These are simple rules of sanitation and should be followed in handling all animals, including your dog, cat, and hamster.

KEEPING YOUR ANIMAL COMFORTABLE

Never leave your animal where he is exposed to rain, wind, or a hot sun with no means of escape from them. Always provide him with animal blankets so that he can cover himself if he feels uncomfortable.

Place his cage or box so that most of it is in the shade but there is a sunny side or corner where he can lie in the sun if he wishes. Give him a choice. But watch to see that he is not in full sun later, as the day passes.

Nocturnal, or night, animals, such as raccoons and possums, can be harmed by bright sun and need sheltered places. Even squirrels prefer partial shade and do not lie in full sun except in the early morning, when the sunshine is mild and the woods are still chilly from dew.

In spite of their heavy winter coats, furry wild animals may develop pneumonia or other winter ills if they become wet and chilled. Notice that you rarely see furry animals out in unpleasant weather. Unless they are extremely hungry or thirsty, they will hole up until the rainstorm, blizzard, or heat spell has passed.

So do not expose your animal to weather conditions that could hurt him.

Keep him out of drafts.

When we use a wire cage for a small animal, we put in it a box or basket of "blankets" in which he can sleep or take refuge when he wishes. This is a good way to keep him comfortable.

FEEDING MEASUREMENTS

2 tablespoons = 1 ounce
3 teaspoons = 1 tablespoon or ½ ounce
½ dropper = about ¼ teaspoon

Half droppers. Half droppers are never quite the same and never quite accurate, but can be estimated as follows, without harm to the little animal:

4 half droppers = 1 teaspoon
8–10 half droppers = about 2½ teaspoons
10–12 half droppers = about 1 tablespoon

POSSUM CARE

Since possums are rather dull-witted and therefore less fearful than other woods animals, they are not as likely to go into shock from being handled when they are babies. Nevertheless, they should be handled no more than is necessary, and always gently. Read and follow the directions for Immediate Emergency Care (page 88) if the baby seems very young and unusually weak.

Keep the little possum lightly covered and comfortably warm. Remember that light can hurt his eyes very much, so do not expose him to lamps or sunlight. Keep his box or cage darkened during the day by covering it with a cloth or newspaper in such a way that he still has plenty of air.

Food. The formula used must depend on the baby possum's age. I had one orphaned possum so little that when he curled up into a ball for a nap, he was no bigger than an English walnut. For a very young and tiny possum, use the following food:

FORMULA 1

1 cup whole milk (scalded but not boiled) or 8 half-droppers

Cool to lukewarm and feed 2 teaspoons every 3 hours, day and night, using a medicine dropper. Keep the scalded milk in a covered container in the refrigerator and be sure it is fresh and sweet. Warm to feed.

FORMULA 2

Use this after a week of feeding the above or for a baby possum that seems strong and lively from the first and is perhaps a bit older.

1 cup whole milk (scalded but not boiled)
dry baby cereal, such as Gerber's

Cool the milk to lukewarm. Add enough dry cereal to make a "sloppy" mixture fairly thick, but still thin enough to go through a medicine dropper. Feed every 3 hours during the day, giving about 8–10 half droppers each time, which will be about 2½ teaspoons. Keep mixture refrigerated between meals. Warm to lukewarm each time.

FORMULA 3

If the possum is not a baby just out of the pouch, but is about the size of a chipmunk, use this formula. You can use it, too, for a possum you have had at least 3 weeks and have already fed Formulas 1 and 2.

1 cup whole milk (scalded but not boiled)
1 raw egg yolk (small)
dry baby cereal, such as Gerber's

Cool the milk and add the egg yolk, mixing thoroughly. Add the cereal as for Formula 2 and feed 1 tablespoon (10–12 half droppers) with a medicine dropper every 3 hours for 5 feedings. Refrigerate between meals and warm each time. The possum will soon take this formula by himself from a flat ashtray or can lid.

Important! Remember that Formula 3 is for *possums, never* for baby squirrels or other small animals that cannot tolerate egg yolk.

Feeding. The easiest way to warm a refrigerated formula is to pour what you will need into a small container and set this in a bowl of hot water until it is lukewarm.

101

Wrap the baby in a feeding blanket (or washcloth) while giving him his formula. Hold him gently. Do not be alarmed if he snarls or hisses at first. This is his warning to an enemy and will stop when he comes to realize that you are his friend. Remember that all possums have poor eyesight, and yours must learn to recognize you by your scent and voice.

Of course, feedings will depend largely on the baby possum's condition at the time. Little Joe was so weak and close to death when I got him that I had to force the first small feedings down him.

I have since had a baby possum named Jasper, who was even younger. He had been taken from his mother's pouch after she was killed by a car and was not accustomed to opening his mouth. For the first small feedings I had to hold his mouth open while Lee dropped the formula into it. But in two days Jasper had learned to open his mouth and eat.

Later foods. After you have fed the possum for at least 3 weeks, start giving him a little bread and milk. Gradually feed scraped apple, pieces of apple, white grapes, small pieces of pear. He will probably eat some *dry* dog food (puppy type) and will love bits of leftover chicken or vegetables.

I was never able to interest Little Joe in eggs, though some possums do like eggs, cooked and raw. Out-of-doors they search the leaves and grass for snails, earthworms, crawfish, beetles, crickets, grasshoppers, and some kinds of bugs. Let your possum find his own, as you may not know which could be harmful.

All possums love fruit and eat a great deal of it when they can find it. They also like certain kinds of nuts and some will eat raisins.

Being night animals, they prefer to eat after dark. They like a small snack around dusk and another around midnight. But when food is available, they eat their main meal around dawn. As Little Joe grew older, I left his pan on the sun porch at night and let him eat when he pleased. He usually woke up after sunset.

Here is a list of the things most possums like best:

POSSUM FOODS

Dry dog food (use the puppy type for young animals)
Cut-up meat, especially leftover chicken (no pork)
Bread and milk
Vegetables, cooked and raw, and raw tops
Eggs, cooked and raw

FRUIT

Apples	Raisins	Pawpaws
White grapes	Pears	Ground cherries
Haw apples	Persimmons	Cherries

(Jasper, my third possum, loved creamy soups and lapped them up the way a kitten laps milk. Some possums will eat canned dog food, but *do not* give them the all-meat type even if it is labeled "for puppies." It is much too rich for little possums and will make them sick.

NUTS

English walnuts

pecans

beechnuts

(The possum will crack these open without any help from you.)

Now and then give him a clean bone to gnaw.
See Possum Feeding Chart at end of chapter.

Water. Possums need a great deal of water, which is why they like to live near streams. At first Little Joe refused to take water from a medicine dropper, but this is not unusual. I kept water in front of him at all times, however, putting it in an ashtray too heavy for him to upset, and he was soon drinking it freely.

Bathing. Because of the musk under their skin, possums in captivity can become very smelly and will need regular baths.

Possums do wash themselves, like a cat, and in the wild are washed by rain or in the streams where they drink and swim. But you will need to bathe yours at least once a month.

I made Little Joe's bathwater lukewarm, used a washcloth, and a mild *soap*. (No animal should *ever* be bathed with detergent or shampoo, as this will dry his skin and cause it to become sore and itchy.)

I covered one side of the basement sink with a terry towel so that Little Joe could hold onto its rough surface. Then I stood him up in the sudsy water. His little hands held tight to the edge while I sponged him clean, scrubbed his hands and feet, and washed his little white face, being careful to keep the soap away from his eyes and mouth. Then I put him down on a bath mat and washed his tail.

Washing a possum's tail. Wring some of the water out of the washcloth. Then lightly grasp the base of the tail (next to the body) with the soapy washcloth in your hand. The possum will walk slowly away, pulling his tail through the cloth. Keep this up until the tail is clean, then rinse him.

After his bath I rolled Joe in a thick towel and rubbed him gently but thoroughly. He was very patient about this and never complained or tried to bite me. Afterward I brushed his fur, which shone like silver. Then I put him back in his cage and covered him for a nap. No longer did he smell like musk. He smelled like Camay!

In winter, when I was afraid he might catch cold, I dried him with the hose of my hair dryer, turning it to its lowest point so that the air was just warm.

A possum should not be bathed while he is a baby, but only when he is about half grown.

Should you decide to bathe a possum of your own, do this only after he has gone to the toilet. Otherwise he may soil the water while you are washing him because water is the toilet they seek out in the wild whenever possible.

Exercise. Possums love to poke around orchards and lawns and woodsy places after dark. We always watched Little Joe carefully and carried a flashlight so that we could switch it on and find him if we lost him in the shadows. We never let him explore a tree trunk too closely, for if he climbed up into the branches, we could not get him down.

Possums love to walk and often walk all night. If you have a screened porch or any other enclosure where a possum will be safe, even a closed room or a basement, let him spend part of his nights there. Leave water and snacks for him.

Vitamins. Ask your vet about Pet Drops for your possum. The usual dose is vitamin liquid to the first mark on the dropper, daily or once a week, as he advises.

Perhaps this will not be needed at all. And remember: *never* give it to babies!

Toilet habits. A possum will instinctively use thick newspapers whether they are in his cage or on some sort of floor space. Since his droppings are quite offensive, you will want to roll up the papers and dispose of them at once.

Important. *Never* put two possums in one cage. They may become quite ferocious and one may hurt or even kill the other.

Releasing the possum. A possum may be released as soon as he is six months old or after he has been on solid food for a while. Do not put him in an area where he is likely to be found and harmed by dogs or where he can easily wander into street and highway traffic. Release him in a woodsy, protected area close to water, perhaps in a state park or wildlife sanctuary. Possums are quite hardy and self-reliant and quite able to care for themselves in a place of this kind.

Read "Releasing Your Animal," on page 150 before setting him free.

POSSUM FEEDING CHART· (Read chapter for fuller explanations.)

AGE	*FOOD*	*DIRECTIONS*
Very young and weak	Emergency formula (rarely necessary)	2–5 drops every 2–4 hours for 24 hours.
Very young and small	Formula 1	8 half droppers (2 teaspoons) every 3 hours, day and night.
After 1 week of Formula 1 when baby is stronger and livelier	Formula 2	8–10 half droppers (about 2½ teaspoons) every 3 hours for 5 feedings.
After feeding baby for 3 weeks, when he is about the size of a small chipmunk	Formula 3	10–12 half droppers (1 tablespoon) every 3 hours for 5 feedings.
If the possum is getting along well on Formula 3, gradually *add* these	Scraped apple Small pieces of apple White grapes Pieces of fresh pear Bread and milk Formula 3	Try feeding him these in small amounts, not all at once. Peel the fruit.
Gradually add these and discontinue formula	Dry dog food (puppy type) Leftover chicken and vegetables	Small amount (may like). Small amount (may like).
When the possum seems to be doing well on solid food, he may be considered weaned	Dry dog food (puppy type) Cut-up meat, especially chicken (no pork), raw liver bread and butter (or chicken fat)	Main meal: dawn. Snacks: around dusk and midnight.

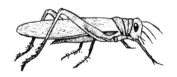

Once he is weaned, you may vary the possum's diet with the following foods:

FOOD	DIRECTIONS
Fruits Cherries Apples White grapes Haw apples Raisins Pears Papaws Persimmons Ground cherries	Possums are especially fond of apples, grapes, persimmons, and Bing cherries. Some will eat raisins.
Nuts English walnuts Pecans Beechnuts	Shells are good for his teeth.
Eggs Raw and scrambled	Some possums like them; some do not.
Bone A clean bone	Occasionally. Excellent for his teeth.
Out-of-Doors Leaves and grass Snails Earthworms Crawfish Beetles Crickets Grasshoppers	He will catch these on his own.
Water (Important)	Fresh and clean, at all times.

107

GROUNDHOG CARE

Only if a young groundhog is *really* lost or his mother is dead should he ever be picked up and taken home.

A little groundhog does not come out of the den until he is old enough to hunt greens, to romp and wrestle with his brothers and sisters, and to learn safety lessons from his mother. He may wander away while hunting food, so the fact that he is alone rarely means that he cannot find his way back to the den or that he is an orphan.

Food. But if a baby groundhog does need help, follow the directions in Immediate Emergency Care, page 88. Keep him covered and comfortably warm. If he is very small and weak, you may have to start his feedings with a medicine dropper, but a pet bottle should be used as soon as possible.

FORMULA

1 cup whole milk (scalded but not boiled)
1 level tablespoon white Karo syrup (use measuring spoon)

Feed him 8 *half* droppers every 3 hours, day and night, until he opens his eyes. (If he will nurse the pet bottle, fill it to *just under* the first mark.) This will be about 2 teaspoons.

After his eyes are open, add dry baby cereal (such as Gerber's) to the formula to make a "sloppy" mixture and feed it to him during the day, using 8–10 *half* droppers each time, or 2½ teaspoons. Refrigerate the formula between meals and warm it each time, making sure it is fresh and sweet. He will soon take it from a flat ashtray or a can lid.

A baby groundhog opens his eyes when he is about 4 weeks old. He is usually still in the den at that age. Do not be worried if your baby animal doesn't open both his eyes at the same time. We have had many animals that opened one eye on Tuesday, for instance, and the other on Wednesday. Even if he *starts* to open both eyes at once, they may not be fully open for several days.

Later foods. About 2 weeks after the little groundhog's eyes are open, give him scraped apple along with his formula, then pieces of apple and small pieces of banana. He will soon ignore the formula and should be on completely solid food after he is 3 or 4 months old.

> *meat* (not pork), including leftover chicken
> *dog food*, dry and chunky
> *greens*, especially clover, plantain, and lettuce
> *fruit,* pears, oranges, apples, peaches, bananas
> *vegetables* such as raw corn, sweet potatoes, and carrots
> *grain,* sunflower seed, wild birdseed, wheat, and oats
> *bread,* preferably whole wheat or rye
> *rabbit pellets,* some *hamster food*

Sugar loved a sweet treat once in a while, such as a cookie, small peanut cluster, or her favorite fig bar.

English walnuts, preferably unshelled, are good for your   109 groundhog if fed sparingly and will help keep his teeth from growing too long. So will hard bread and dry dog food. All gnawing animals (rodents) must keep their teeth ground down, for if the teeth become too long, the animals suffer great pain, cannot eat, and will starve to death.

See Groundhog Feeding Chart at end of chapter.

Water. Keep clean, fresh water before your groundhog at all times.

Bathing. Never try to bathe a groundhog, even a baby. He will clean his own coat and take his own baths. Should he get some sticky food on his coat, he will probably clean it off by himself. If not, you can wipe it off with a damp cloth, but do not use soap and do not put him in water.

Exercise. Groundhogs are extremely playful and like to romp indoors and out. They are likely to become excited, and since their teeth and claws are sharp, they can hurt you without realizing it. So it is best to wear gloves and long sleeves when you play with them.

You can take your groundhog for a walk, not along the street, where he might become frightened and dash away, but in some place where he can enjoy nibbling green shoots and plants, such as a protected lawn, a quiet park, or a meadow. If he should climb a tree, wait patiently for him to come down. Unlike squirrels, a groundhog does not stay in a tree for long.

Molting. A groundhog molts (sheds his old fur) once a year. The molt starts at his face, also at his tail, and works toward the middle. The old, rough hair falls out and sleek new hair comes in. The molt is always finished before hibernation.

Release. Groundhogs are extremely independent and want a life of their own. So try to realize from the start that no matter how much your groundhog seems attached to you, he will always love freedom more. Be prepared to let him go back to the wild when the time comes. He should be released before the end of his first summer in some quiet place near a woods or meadow (or both) where he can easily find water and where he will be reasonably safe from traffic and hunters. Nature will show him how to prepare a cozy den for winter.

Read "Releasing Your Animal" on page 150.

GROUNDHOG FEEDING CHART (Read chapter for fuller explanations.)

AGE	FOOD	DIRECTIONS
Young, small, weak (eyes closed)	Milk formula	8 half droppers (2 teaspoons) every 3 hours, day and night, until eyes open.
After eyes open (about 4 weeks old)	Cereal formula	10–12 half droppers (about 2½ teaspoons) every 3 hours during the day or 5 feedings.
2 weeks after eyes open	Milk formula plus: Scraped apple Pieces of apple Small pieces of banana White grapes	Increase solid food gradually in small amounts while decreasing formula.
Solid food (3–4 months of age)	Meat (not pork) including leftover chicken Fruit (above) Dog food, dry and chunky Greens, especially clover, lettuce, plantain	Feed gradually until baby is weaned from milk formula.

CHICKAREE (RED SQUIRREL) CARE

First of all, follow the directions in Immediate Emergency Care. Be extremely careful in handling a baby chickaree (a kind of red squirrel). They are very tiny, delicate, and easily injured. Handle a chickaree no more than is absolutely necessary.

Food. After following Immediate Emergency Care, give the following formula, first with a medicine dropper, then with a NIP Pet Nurser made especially for small animals. Never put more than one feeding at a time into the bottle. Overfeeding the baby will kill it.

FORMULA

1 cup whole milk (scalded, but not boiled)
1 scant tablespoon of white Karo syrup (use measuring spoon)

Use a measuring spoon in preparing the formula. Before feeding it, cool it to lukewarm, trying a few drops on your wrist, as for a human baby. Then feed it to the chickaree every 3 hours, *a little at a time* (4 or 5 half droppers). Continue this amount until he is fully furred out. Refrigerate the formula between meals, keeping it covered, and heat the feeding to lukewarm each time.

After the baby is furred out and his eyes have been open for about a week, add dry baby cereal (such as Gerber's) to the formula to make a "sloppy mixture." Feed this every 4 hours during the day, a bit less than a tablespoon at a time. You can feed it from a medicine dropper at first, but the chickaree will soon be taking it from a container such as a flat ashtray or a can lid. Wipe any residue from his face with a soft damp cloth. Gradually add nut balls (p. 146), white seedless grapes (1 per feeding), and a little scraped apple.

All squirrels are delicate and must be carefully fed. If the chickaree shows symptoms of diarrhea, reduce the amount of white Karo until the bowels are regulated. Do this at once, as diarrhea can be fatal.

After the chickaree is weaned, he may be introduced *gradually* to fruit, greens, and other foods. All chickarees are very fond of sunflower seeds and dry corn, but should be allowed only *one sunflower seed and one grain of corn per day*. Some like meal worms. Some will eat bits of raw hamburger. They will not all like the same thing.

See Chickaree Feeding Chart at end of chapter.

Water. Keep fresh water before the chickaree at all times. A small, flat, heavy ashtray makes the best container.

Housing. At first a small (open) box supplied with pet blankets will do, then a cage about the size of a canary cage. After that your chickaree will need a large parakeet flight cage to give him room for play.

Furniture. If twigs are chosen for furniture or for a swing, use apple or maple twigs.

Never give any animal bark, fruit, or leaves unless you know what you are doing. Among poisonous items are cherry twigs, certain locust blooms, and many leaves, including peach leaves.

The midden. The midden (or storehouse) is very important to the chickaree, who often saves part of his meals for it. A long soft cloth will make a fine midden. He will design it to suit himself.

CHICKAREE (RED SQUIRREL) FEEDING CHART

(Read chapter for fuller explanations.)

AGE	FOOD	DIRECTIONS
Young and weak (eyes not open, no fur)	Emergency formula	2–5 drops every 2–4 hours for first 24 hours.
Very young, until eyes are open and animal is furred out (eyes open in 27 days)	Milk formula	4–5 half droppers (about 1 teaspoon) every 3 hours, day and night.
Furred out and eyes open for about a week	Cereal formula	10–12 half droppers (about 1 tablespoon) every 4 hours during the day for 4 feedings. As soon as possible, feed this from flat, heavy ashtray.
	Nut balls (see Recipes)	Very small, add gradually.
	Scraped apple (½ teaspoon)	Add gradually.

After five to six weeks, the chickaree will be weaned. The cereal formula can be discontinued. His diet can be varied with the foods on this list. Give two feedings per day.

FOOD	DIRECTIONS
	Determine what your animal likes best. Then offer these foods in small amounts, using a variety each day.

Fruits
Apples
Oranges
Bananas
Melon
Pears
Peaches
Grapes
Berries, especially mulberries

Peel oranges, bananas, and
melons.

Greens
Clover, red, never white
Lettuce
Redbud bloom (in spring)

Feed only small amounts of
lettuce and redbud bloom.

Cereals
Raw wheat or oats
Sunflower seeds
Dry corn

A few grains at a time.
1 per day.
1 grain per day.

Nuts
Pecans
English walnuts

Serve in halves.

Pet food
Birdseed
Hamster food

Very small amounts.

For teeth
Hard toast
Zwieback

These help to keep his teeth
from growing too long.

Water
(Important)

Fresh and clean, at all times.

RACCOON CARE

Food. If a baby raccoon is tiny and weak, he may be started on the emergency formula. (See page 90)

We followed this with the usual whole-milk-and-white-Karo mixture, but this did not agree with Ceecee at that age, as it had with other woods babies. He developed diarrhea, which is dangerous because it can quickly kill a small animal. So we used the following formula instead, feeding him *every 3 hours, day and night.*

1½ teaspoons of skimmed milk (scalded, not boiled)
3 drops of Kaopectate (available at drugstores)

Measure this into a pet nursing bottle and shake it well before giving it. If you have no bottle as yet, mix it thoroughly and give it with a medicine dropper.

After the diarrhea is really under control, use the regular formula:

FORMULA
1 cup of whole milk (scalded, but not boiled)
1 level tablespoon white Karo (use measuring spoon)

Keep covered in the refrigerator between meals. Warm each feeding to lukewarm.

118

Starting with 2½ teaspoons, we fed Ceecee this formula *every 3 hours, day and night*. Gradually the feedings were changed (according to whether Ceecee woke up and demanded them) to 4 times a day, morning, noon, late afternoon, and bedtime. The amount of formula was gradually increased, so that by the time he was 2 months old he was taking from 1–1¾ ounces per feeding.

Ceecee was 3 or 4 months old before he was willing to give up his bottle. He then began eating apples, grapes, bananas, leftover chicken and other kinds of solid food, but not too much at a time.

Growing. Most baby raccoons open their eyes when they are 18–20 days old.

Although they cry a good deal, it only means that they are exercising their lungs. But always check carefully to make sure they are not soiled, too hot, too cold, or past their feeding time.

Their permanent teeth grow in between August and October of their first year.

Young raccoons usually stay near the mother until the spring after they are born, though some may leave the previous fall. Often when a litter breaks up, the raccoons live and hunt in pairs for a while, though an adult raccoon prefers to live alone.

The mother teaches them lessons in hunting, foraging, fishing, hiding, denning, and how to escape enemies, which (unfortunately) *you* cannot do.

Bathing. Raccoons take their own baths. Do not try to bathe them, as this will frighten them, and shampoo, both soap and detergent, will harm their fur and skin.

119

After weaning, about four months of age, vary the diet with the following foods:

FOOD	DIRECTIONS
Fruits	Feed one piece at a time.
Pears	
Grapes	
Oranges	
Apples	
Peaches	
Bananas	Feed only ¼ medium
(Most groundhogs are especially fond of bananas.)	banana, small pieces at a time.
Cereals	
Wild bird seed	
Sunflower seed	
Wheat (raw)	
Oats (raw)	
Bread	Prefers rye or whole wheat
Some hamster food	bread, but likes white bread, too.
Sweet treats	Feed sweet treats sparingly
Cookie or cupcake	once in a while.
Small peanut cluster	
Fig bar	
For teeth	These will keep teeth from
Unshelled English walnuts	growing too long.
Hard bread	
Dry Dog food	
Dog biscuits	
Water	Fresh and clean at all times.
(Important)	

Sounds. A tiny raccoon who has lost its mother will call to her with a sound something like that of a locust or tree frog. Later he "talks" to his mother, and she answers him with a soft *ptrrrrr . . . ptrrrrr* sound. At times he cries like a baby.

Often, in the fall, raccoons may be heard "singing" on quiet, moonlit nights. This is a soft, high, trembling sound which could easily be mistaken for a screech owl. They call to one another in this way as if being friendly and sociable.

Later Foods. In the wild raccoons eat many kinds of food which they hunt and find at night. They fish in streams with their active little hands and turn rocks over to find minnows, crawfish, frogs, and the insects that live around water.

A raccoon eats garden insects also, grasshoppers, spiders, beetles, and others. He is fond of bees and will catch them in his hand and shove them quickly into his mouth. Since he is attracted to all sweets, he may eat both bees and honey from a hive.

Raccoons like the flesh of geese, ducks, chickens, and often eat game that is shot and lost by hunters. Among Ceecee's favorite foods were meat, vegetables, cereal, nuts, and fruit.

See Raccoon Feeding Chart at end of chapter.

Ceecee was very fond of nuts in the shell and seemed to enjoy opening them by himself.

Like all raccoons, he liked sweets, so we sometimes treated him to a jelly sandwich or one of jelly with a thin layer of peanut butter. We would give him a cookie or a cut-up cupcake, but his favorite of all sweets was marshmallows.

Raccoons like bread and often come to our garden for pieces from the loaves we buy at "second day" places. They prefer dark bread.

Ceecee loved hard-boiled eggs. And sometimes he ate dry dog food, but he was not very fond of it.

After he grew up, we fed him one meal a day, usually late at night.

Water. Keep fresh water for your raccoon in a large, heavy red-clay saucer, the kind made to hold flowerpots, or the bowl from a birdbath.

Raccoons sometimes soften food in the water before eating it, but not always. They do drink a good deal of water, however, and often wash playthings in it, such as small stones. Raccoons love to wash and play with small, solid objects, but do not give them anything easily broken, such as plastic, which could hurt them very much. They are especially fond of bright-colored toys and will play with balls and small erasers.

Dens. A raccoon seems to feel safest when sleeping in a small space and usually makes his den in a hollow tree or limb. In the country he may live in a haystack, a rocky hole, a groundhog den, or some other dry, hidden place if no trees are available.

The sketch on page 123 shows the boxlike den which Lee built for Ceecee and which was placed on the sun porch. Here Ceecee slept curled up in "animal blankets" most of the day.

A raccoon may sleep curled up like a puppy, on his tummy or his back. In the wild he sometimes sleeps on a branch or in the fork of a tree in any position he finds safe and comfortable.

While a raccoon does not hibernate like a groundhog, he does sleep more in cold weather. Like most woods animals, he snores loudly.

Molting. Raccoons molt (shed) from March through May. During this time their coats may look shabby and ragged and their tails scrubby and thin. Their coats are always lighter and cooler in summer, but grow heavy and handsome in the fall. In December their coats are so thick that the raccoons look like small bears, and their tails are round and fluffy.

Age. Raccoons have lived as long as 14 years in captivity and as long as 12 years in the wild, though 12 years is probably an unusual life span for them. They may die of illness or injury, and many are killed by hunters for their fur and by hunters' dogs.

Release. By the time a raccoon is old enough to find a mate he is ready for his freedom.

Though a few (very few) raccoons remain sweet and gentle at this time, most of them become cross, stubborn, unfriendly, and even quite dangerous.

Do not feel shocked or angry or hurt if your raccoon suddenly snarls and barks at you or snaps at you, and *never* try to punish him for this. Remember that it is his nature to want a place of his own in the wild and a mate, and nothing else is so important to him now.

Do not think of him as "mean" or "ungrateful" but only as a wild animal doing what Nature has told him to do. Release him in a protected area (page 150) while he is still young enough to adjust and while the weather is warm and pleasant.

In spite of their sudden hostile, stubborn, and sometimes frightening behavior, raccoons are very much attached to their human friends and their first homes and do not entirely forget them. Country people who have released a raccoon in the woods on their own land may find that he keeps coming back to the house at night for visits and for food and will answer with a soft whine when his name is called. I know of one female raccoon who, two years after being released, brought her babies back to live in the tree near the farmhouse where she had been raised and had played when she was small.

We once released a young raccoon named Cookie in our
own wooded acreage, where she promptly went to live in an oak

tree. In a few weeks she had made the acquaintance of one or two other raccoons from the neighborhood, who had dropped in on moonlit nights and still do. From the window we would watch their riotous games of rolling, tumbling, racing, and somersaulting through the garden.

After seven years Cookie is still with us. Sometimes we find her lying on our roof in the sun on chilly mornings. On autumn nights we hear her "singing" from the tree outside our bedroom window. She drinks from the birdbath on the ground, pokes around the garden for grubs and insects, helps herself to fruit and nuts from the trees. At times we leave stale bread or dry dog food for her.

Many times, late at night, I have heard her small black hand fumbling at the patio door, trying to come into the room where I am reading, looking for a snack. When this happens, we go to the door and give her some sort of treat. But we never bring her into the house now, for even though a woods animal has been raised indoors, walls fill him with panic once he has known freedom.

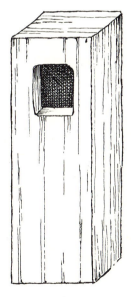

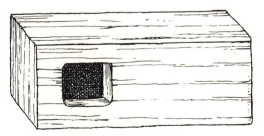

Coon Shelter
which Lee built for Ceecee. Upright it was a "tree trunk." Horizontal it became a "log." In winter, when Ceecee slept a great deal, the log was preferred.

Dimensions. Length: 36″. Width: 18″. Depth: 15″. The opening, 5″ from the top, was 6″ by 9″.

RACCOON FEEDING CHART (Read chapter for fuller explanations.)

AGE	FOOD	DIRECTIONS
Tiny and weak, eyes not open	Emergency formula	2–5 drops every 2–4 hours for the first 24 hours.
Very small	Milk formula (Should diarrhea develop, use directions on page 95)	10 half droppers, or 2½ teaspoons, measured on bottle.
Small, eyes open, sleeps through the night (eyes open in 18–20 days)	Milk formula	1–1¾ ounces, about 3 tablespoons, as indicated on bottle; 4 times a day, morning, noon, afternoon, bedtime.
Start weaning at 3–4 months by decreasing formula and adding solid food	Leftover poultry (no bones, no pork) apple (small pieces) Grapes (a few) Banana (small piece)	Raccoons are especially fond of chicken. A little at a time; use at each feeding.

When fully weaned (about 5 months), vary diet with foods listed here.

FOOD	DIRECTIONS
Meats Leftover poultry Hamburger Other meats, but not bones and no pork	Feed once a day, preferably in the evening.

124

Vegetables
Carrots
Sweet potatoes
Fresh corn
Lettuce

Small amounts, lightly cooked.

Fruits
Berries
Cherries
Persimmons
Plums
Oranges
Apples
Melons

Feed all fruits sparingly but keep
them in the diet regularly.
Peel oranges and melons.

Cereals
Sugar-coated boxed
cereal, preferably puffed wheat.

A few grains at a time.

Nuts
English walnuts
Pecans

The raccoon will crack them.

Sweet treats
Peanut butter and jelly sandwich
Cut-up cupcake
Cookie
Marshmallows

Thin peanut butter.
Feed treats occasionally.

Eggs
Boiled or scrambled

Feed frequently.

Water
(Important)

Fresh and clean at all
times. Can be offered in a large,
flat, heavy container such as a
flower pot saucer.

125

COTTONTAIL RABBIT CARE

Food. Baby rabbits are delicate little creatures and must be handled gently and carefully. If yours is quite small, you may have to start his feedings with a medicine dropper. As soon as possible, use a NIP Pet Nurser, with the bottle filled to just under the first mark for each feeding. This would be 8–10 *half* droppers, or about 2½ teaspoons.

We have had success in feeding baby rabbits and some other tiny animals with Enfamil, a ready-mixed formula for human babies which can be bought at most drugstores. If this is not available where you live, use the basic formula (below) for baby animals:

MILK FORMULA

1 cup whole milk (scalded but not boiled)
1 level tablespoon of white Karo syrup (use measuring spoon)

Remember that rabbits can die very quickly from overfeeding. Give him the formula, as directed, every 4 hours through the day until he is 2 weeks old, gradually increasing it to ½ ounce, or a full tablespoon. Refrigerate the mixture between feedings, but have it lukewarm when it is fed, and be sure it is fresh and sweet. Keep it covered while it is stored.

A rabbit's mouth looks surprisingly large when it is open, but when it is closed, it is so small that it is hard to find. Examine the baby and locate its mouth before you start feeding it, or you will be trying to force the nipple into its nose.

Later foods. At the age of 2 or 3 weeks (when he starts to nibble) you may add tiny bits of bread to the formula, and if possible give the little rabbit some red-clover blossoms. Decrease the formula as he learns to eat.

As soon as he is eating well, you can add other foods. See Cottontail Feeding Chart at end of chapter.

If you know the following wild plants when you see them, gather them for him in warm months:

dandelion leaves	sorrel (sour grass)
chickweed	chicory leaves
plantain	lamb's-quarters

Beware, however, of greens that are too wet and juicy, as they may cause him to have diarrhea. If this happens, decrease or omit the greens for a little while.

Do not overfeed your rabbit. Keep a salt tablet or a small lump of salt in his cage for him to lick. He should have 3 feedings a day. Most cottontails sleep a good deal during the day and like to feed at dusk, in the night, or very early in the morning. It is a good idea to leave one feeding in his cage when you go to bed.

Water. Have clean, fresh water before him at all times, even though he may not seem to drink much of it.

Eyes. A baby rabbit's eyes open when he is 7 days old.   127

Teeth. A rabbit's teeth grow fast, so he will need to gnaw something to keep them the proper length. Give him stout twigs from a fruit tree, preferably an apple tree. (Even a baby rabbit can bite hard!)

Exercise. As soon as the rabbit is on solid food, let him play around the cage area by hopping, leaping, and running. If you handle him every day, pet him, and talk to him, he will probably be quite tame. Never grasp him suddenly or hold him too tight. *Never lift him by his ears!* Lift him with one hand grasping the back of his neck and the other hand under his haunches, as though he were sitting on your palm.

Toilet habits. A rabbit's droppings are like small round seeds. Provide thick papers for him to use. Sometimes rabbits pass a certain kind of pellet which contains Vitamin B and which they will later eat. Do not be shocked by this. Remember that Nature gives each animal its own means of survival.

Release. Since a cottontail rabbit can usually be released when he is 2 months old, you can keep him in a wire cage or in a small box enclosed in a reasonably large cage until he is ready to go. Provide him with "animal blankets" and change them daily, just as you change the papers that line the cage. While he is small, heat at least one corner of the box with a heating pad, as described in General Care on page 89–90.

All cottontails living out-of-doors need a shelter for both summer and winter, hot or cold weather, wet or dry. This should be a woodsy area with grass to provide nests and "resting forms" for them, enough shrubbery to hide them from enemies, and enough brush to keep them warm and dry.

Release your cottontail in a thick growth or cover while

the weather is warm and pleasant. This may be in a hedge, in deep grass, or in the woods, but should be near a meadow where he can find the food he likes, such as clover. Sometimes a rabbit can be released in a park, especially a state park where the park naturalist can help you find the proper place for him.

Read "Releasing Your Animal" on page 150.

COTTONTAIL FEEDING CHART (Read chapter for fuller explanations.)

AGE	*FOOD*	*DIRECTIONS*
Very young, up to 3 weeks old	Milk formula (or Enfamil)	8–10 half droppers (2½ teaspoons) every 4 hours during the day).
After 2–3 weeks (when he starts to nibble)	Milk formula (or Enfamil) with tiny bits of soft bread added	Increase to ½ ounce or 1 full tablespoon. Decrease formula as rabbit learns to eat.
	Clover blossoms	When he starts to nibble.

After the animal is eating well, you can vary his diet with the following, until he is released.

FOOD	DIRECTIONS
Formula with bread added	Feed twice a day and leave food in cage for night feeding. Discontinue this as rabbit loses interest in it.

Vegetables
Bits of fresh spinach
A little lettuce
Bits of fresh beet tops
Thinly sliced carrot pieces

Fruits
Thinly sliced apple bits

Pet Food
Birdseed
Hamster food (green pellets)
Green rabbit pellets

Fresh Wild Plants
Dandelion greens
Chickweed
Plantain
Sorrel (sour grass)
Chicory
Lamb's quarters
Small violet leaves

| **Salt**
Salt tablet or small lump of salt. | Keep in cage. |
| **Water**
(Important) | At all times, may drink very little. |

FOX SQUIRREL CARE

Food. A baby squirrel must be kept warm, dry, and quiet.

If he is extremely small and weak, use the emergency formula for the first 24 hours. If not (or after that), use the regular baby formula:

FORMULA

1 cup whole milk (scalded but *not* boiled)
1 level tablespoon white Karo (use measuring spoon)

No matter *who* may recommend it, *never* give a baby fox squirrel a formula with egg yolk in it. He will die if you do.

Use a NIP Pet Nurser if possible, and fill it to the first mark. (This is 2½ teaspoons, or 8–10 half-filled medicine droppers.)

Try the formula on your wrist to make sure it is lukewarm, then squeeze the bottle into the baby's mouth, but be careful you don't squirt it, or the milk may enter his lungs. A bottle with too large a hole in the nipple will feed too fast and choke him, so watch this carefully. In a short time he will hold the bottle in both his hands while he is fed.

132   Lift him gently by slipping your hand under him or by tak-

ing hold of him across his back, at the shoulders. Never, *never* try to lift or catch a squirrel by the tail.

While giving him his bottle, hold him gently but firmly in a feeding blanket or washcloth. (Baby squirrels are very slippery.) Feed him *every 3 hours, day and night,* until he is completely furred out. Then feed him every 3 hours during the day, *gradually* increasing the amount of formula. Even when he is 10 weeks old, however, he should not take more than 1 ounce (2 tablespoons) at a feeding, as overfeeding can kill him. Always put him back in his bed after the feeding.

Baby squirrels that are not fed on time may start nursing one another's bodies and cause serious injuries.

After eyes are open. Fox squirrels usually open their eyes when they are 6 weeks old. After their eyes have been opened for a few days, start them on cereal.

CEREAL FORMULA

Mix the usual whole-milk-and-white-Karo formula. Then add dry baby cereal (such as Gerber's) to make a "sloppy" gruel. Feed this through a medicine dropper or from a small spoon (not plastic). The animal will soon learn to take it from a flat, heavy ashtray or from a can lid. Feed about 1 ounce at a time.

Baby squirrels are delicate and must be fed *regularly* and *properly.* Do not try to give them nuts until they are older.

Weaning. A squirrel is usually weaned (put entirely on solid food) when he is about 10–11 weeks old. Most fox squirrels will start refusing the formula at this age. Others keep taking it, but develop diarrhea, which indicates (after they are 10 weeks old) that they need more solid food.

133

First solid food.

    1 tablespoon of fresh scraped apple or apple bits
    2 or 3 white grapes, cut in two
    a few cornflakes
    a little hamster food
    nut balls (page146) without egg

Feed sparingly at first until the baby adjusts and you are sure he is doing well. Start with the apple, grapes, and 2 or 3 small nut balls. Gradually add the cornflakes and hamster food, Do not overfeed.

After the squirrel has had these foods for at least a week and seems to be doing well, gradually add items from the Feeding Chart, one or two new ones each day, until you know which he likes best.

When he is well adjusted, change his feedings to 2 a day, a small meal in the early morning and a later one in the late afternoon.

Later foods. The tastes of animals vary as much as the tastes of people. Groany loved watermelon seeds; Ditty wouldn't even try them. Gabby adored tomatoes; none of the other squirrels liked them. Some liked oranges, a bit of banana, or a thin slice of cucumber. Others didn't. Chip loved garlic; others all but ran from it.

See Fox Squirrel Feeding Chart at end of chapter.

Peanuts (which are not really nuts at all) are not good for your squirrel. Feed them sparingly, if at all.

Green corn is not well tolerated by squirrels in captivity, though they like dry corn.

Clover, rose petals, dandelion leaves, and the like should be carefully washed, as they may have been sprayed with some harmful chemical.

Sunflower seeds. Do not feed more than 6 a day. Squirrels fed too freely of sunflower seeds will die from liver trouble at an early age.

A small *ham bone,* not meaty and not sharp, will please your squirrel. He will like the salty taste and the gnawing will help his teeth.

Salt. Squirrels want and need salt. You may provide a salt tablet for them to lick, though some will only bury it. They may also get enough salt by nibbling grains from a dish or from the palm of your hand, from a bone or from hard bread.

Never give a squirrel cheese or anything moldy. Either could kill him.

Breakfast. For a fox squirrel, breakfast should be no more than a grape or a nut. Give him his main meal in late afternoon and do not overfeed him. Remember that what looks like a small snack to you will be a full plate to him.

Vitamins. About once a week offer your squirrel diluted orange juice served in a small, rather flat ashtray.

After he is 12 weeks old, you can start adding some Pet Drops once a week, about 2 drops at a time, if he seems weak.

Water. Keep fresh, clean water before him at all times, using a flat, heavy ashtray as a container or a heavy flowerpot saucer.

Teeth. To keep their teeth from growing too long, squirrels need zwieback, hard bread, and nutshells to gnaw. Give them black walnuts, English walnuts, hickory nuts, or pecans, all slightly cracked. For if the nuts are whole, the squirrels will only bury

135

them somewhere instead of eating them. We gave ours short sticks from apple trees to chew on, too. But choose carefully because the twigs from some trees, such as cherry, are poisonous.

Sleeping. Some squirrels go to sleep early; some do not. Some get up early; others sleep late. They vary as much as people in their habits.

They sleep in a variety of positions, but the favorite seems to be with the head somewhat lower than the body. A squirrel likes lots and lots of loose cover and will arrange it to suit himself.

Vitamins from the woods. Fox squirrels love garden or woods soil and will dig into potted plants if not watched. This will not only damage the plants, but if the pot soil contains fertilizer, it may poison them.

You may prepare a box of soil for them to dig in, as follows: Mix ⅔ loamy woods soil with ⅓ limestone bone meal, which can be found at a feed store. Spread the mixture in a box about 2 inches high and allow the squirrels to explore, dig, and nibble.

Bathing. A squirrel cleans his own coat, washes his face and hands in his own way. Never try to bathe him!

Shock. Because squirrels are very sensitive, they may quickly die of shock if hurt, forcibly restrained, trapped, frightened by loud noises or flashing lights, or handled by strangers. Some squirrels have gone into shock when transported in a car. If they must be taken into an unfamiliar or perhaps frightening place, it is well to cover the cage with a dark cloth or at least a heavy cloth to give them some sense of security. Squirrels may become frightened by the sounds and smells of a veterinary hospital.

Molting. A fox squirrel molts (sheds its old fur) twice a year, in spring and fall. The spring molt usually starts in May and moves from head to tail. You can usually see the molt line very clearly as the old fur falls out and the new comes in. The fall molt starts on the rump and moves in two directions, toward the head and toward the tip of the tail. Molting takes 3 or 4 weeks.

Growing. When the little squirrel is old enough to jump in and out of his box, he is ready for a cage at least 4 x 4 ft. It should be roomy enough to hold his sleeping box and a "resting shelf." This shelf, about 3 inches wide, should stretch across the upper part of the cage, all the way across it. On this narrow shelf he can stretch out to rest or sleep as he would on a limb.

Squirrels are very curious and will get into mischief unless closely watched. Lock yours in his cage when you cannot watch him, as he might chew a light cord, thrust his hand into a socket, upset something which will fall on him, or otherwise get hurt or even killed if left unprotected. He might also chew your furniture.

Squirrels have nimble fingers which can unlatch some cages, unfasten snap clothespins, or untwist twisted wire. The one "latch" they cannot open is a good sturdy dog snap, the kind used to fasten a leash to a collar. You will need more than one of these to secure the cage door. If only one is used, and that in the middle, the squirrel will push the door forward until the wire bulges outward and then climb out the openings at the sides.

Play. As soon as a squirrel begins to roll and tumble in play, give him a washcloth with a knot tied in the middle. He will love playing with it.

He will be delighted, too, with a small box of harmless odds   137 and ends to explore, such as screw-on bottle caps (not plastic), wooden blocks, orange sticks, jingling keys, even paper wads.

Squirrels are interested in motion and like to watch TV. They respond to music and like to hear soft melodies on records.

Release your squirrel every day in some protected indoor area where you can watch him and where he can play without doing much damage by gnawing. A sun porch is ideal. Be sure the area is not too cold, for a squirrel that becomes chilled can develop pneumonia. (Most furry animals try to avoid weather that is extremely cold, rainy, or windy. If they come out at all on such days, it is only to eat, and then they stay out as brief a time as possible. In extreme weather they may not come out for days.)

Hibernation. Squirrels do not really hibernate, as many people seem to think, but are less lively in wintertime and sleep more.

Sounds. Besides the *cr-onnnnk* sound in babyhood and the *waa-waa-waa* call, squirrels make a purring sound like a kitten when petted, bark when annoyed, click their teeth when pleased, growl when hurt or afraid, and chatter warnings. They make other sounds, but these are the most usual.

Toilet habits. A squirrel in the wild will not soil his nest, but will get out and find leaves to use. In the same way he will leave his box and use the paper on the floor of the cage. A squirrel's droppings are small, dark "seeds," which (if he is in good health) are both firm and waxy. They are quite inoffensive. He will wet the paper with a small, equally inoffensive puddle. If his bowels are too loose when he is a baby, *decrease* the Karo in his formula. In some cases it can be discontinued entirely. If not free enough, *increase* the Karo slightly until they seem right.

138

Illness. A squirrel that is ill will usually sit with his head down, refuse food, and make little whispering *mmmmmm* sounds. Keep him warm and comfortable, see that he has fresh water, but do not coax him to eat. If he does not improve, consult a veterinarian—but *only one with experience in treating wild animals, no other!*

The most common reasons for illness are overfeeding, especially of sunflower seeds, becoming wet and chilled, not being covered when a baby or when asleep, lack of fresh vegetables, unnatural foods, such as candy. There are other reasons we do not always understand, for there is much we do not know about their needs.

Do not try to put a bandage on a squirrel if he gets hurt. He will not tolerate a bandage or even a Band-Aid and might go into shock from your efforts.

Do not handle an injured squirrel or any other animal without wearing heavy gloves, for pain will make him bite. As gently as possible, get him into a box, give him water from a medicine dropper if you can, and cover him completely.

Take him to a veterinarian who knows what to do, who understands the type of anesthetic to be used safely on a wild animal and how to keep the animal from panic while he recovers.

Home emergencies. If your squirrel seizes an object you do not want him to have, don't try to take it away. Offer a substitute, and he will drop the first object to take the second.

Should he get out of his cage, do not chase him or try to catch him. This will cause him to panic. Leave his cage open, put food inside, and be patient. He will return to the cage later. If he is very frightened, however, he may hide and return only when the house is really quiet.

139

Never, *never* seize a squirrel by the tail, as much of it will come off and never grow again.

If your squirrel gets out of his box or cage and you cannot wait for him to return at will, you may be able to recover him by tossing a towel or a small blanket over him. This will quiet him and as he huddles under it like a small lump, you can pick him up—*gently*—and put him back where he belongs.

Using a net to recover him is not advisable, as he may become tangled in the mesh and break a delicate bone. In a real emergency use gently and with caution.

Taming. If you want your squirrel to be at ease with you, you *must* take time every day to pet him, handle him, talk to him.

Do *not* teach him to make friends with a dog or to eat from your hand. He should not learn to trust any kind of animal which would harm him after he is released or to trust strangers enough to go close to them.

Releasing your squirrel. It is only right that he should be returned to the wild, but do not let him go until you read "Releasing Your Animal" on page 150 so you will understand how this should be done.

If you live in a large wooded area safely removed from traffic, as in a rural area, it is possible to release your animal gradually. Take his cage to a suitable spot and set it in a safe place. Open the door and allow him to venture in and out as he pleases. If he goes to sleep in his cage at night, close and lock it to protect him from enemies. Then open it next day, keep food and water in it, and let him explore the world around him until he finds a new home and does not return to the cage.

Squirrels released near their first homes may remain in the
area if it seems safe and if there are plenty of trees, as well as

food and water. Some squirrels, after being released, will come back to their human friends when called or for food. Others adjust quickly to their free life and never return.

FOX SQUIRREL FEEDING CHART (Read chapter for fuller explanations.)

AGE	FOOD	DIRECTIONS
Small, weak, eyes closed, almost hairless	Emergency formula	2–5 drops every 2–4 hours for 24 hours.
After 24 hours	Milk formula	4 half droppers every 3 hours, day and night.
About 1 month old, eyes still closed but mostly furred out	Milk formula	8–10 half-filled droppers (2½ teaspoons)—or filled to just under first mark on Nip pet nursing bottle. Feed every 3 hours during day, 5 feedings.
Furred out, even tail. Eyes open for several days. About 7 weeks old.	Cereal formula	2 tablespoons (1 ounce) every 3 hours during the day. Do not feed more than 1 ounce at a time.
Weaned, 10–11 weeks old	First solid food: Fresh scraped apple or apple bits Grapes (cut in two) Nut balls (page 146) Cornflakes Hamster food	3 times a day. 1 tablespoon. 2 or 3, preferably white. 2 or 3. Gradually add: A few. A few pellets.

After one week of solid food, begin to build a well-balanced diet. Not all squirrels like the same food, so try a variety from the list given. Add foods gradually, trying a new one each day.

FOOD	DIRECTIONS
	After squirrel is well-adjusted to solid food, reduce feedings to 2 per day, a small feeding in the morning, a larger one in late afternoon. This should be his schedule from now on.

Vegetables and Greens

Butternut squash and seeds	Too much will cause diarrhea.
Fresh head lettuce	
Dandelion leaves	
Wing of maple tree	In spring.
Redbud bloom	In spring.
Rose petals	Thoroughly washed.
Thin slices of carrot	2 or 3.
Thin slices of cucumber	2 or 3.
Fresh green beans	2 or 3.

Fruits

Grapes
Pears
Peaches
Apples
Berries
Cherries
Watermelon and seeds
Tomatoes

Cereal Foods

Torn-up pieces of bread
Bits of dry, buttered toast — Good for teeth.
Leftover biscuits
Zwieback — Good for teeth.
Leftover doughnuts — 1 small or ½ large.

Protein Foods

Dry dog food (puppy type) — Small amount each meal.
Dog biscuits (puppy type) — 1 each meal.
English walnuts — Break into small pieces and feed several pieces each meal.

Juice

Diluted orange juice — Once a week, may be sweetened with a little honey.

Salt

A small salt block from a pet store — Keep in his cage. He may or may not use it, but it should be offered.

Bone

Small ham bone, no meat — Good for teeth and pleasingly salty.

Water

Fresh clean water, at all times.

Vitamins

After 12 weeks, if the squirrel seems weak and is losing hair, get *Pet Drops* from your veterinarian. This is the *only* vitamin safe for him. — Use 3 drops added to diluted orange juice, once a week.

144

Add these foods when your squirrel is 4 months or older.

FOOD

Corn (preferably dry)

DIRECTIONS

Only a few grains at a time. (Squirrels love green corn, but it sometimes makes the younger ones ill.)

Seeds
Sunflower
Wild birdseed

Not more than 6 per day. (An excess amount of these seeds may cause fatal liver trouble.)

Nuts, slightly cracked
English walnuts
Hickory nuts
Beechnuts
Pecans
Black walnuts

If you give a squirrel a whole, uncracked nut, he will bury it instead of eating it. (Peanuts, which are not true nuts, may do more harm than good.)

RECIPES

Each of these recipes is based on the milk formula given to small, unweaned woods animals.

MILK FORMULA

1 cup of whole milk (scalded but *not* boiled)
1 level tablespoon of white Karo syrup (use measuring spoon)

CEREAL FORMULA

1 cup whole milk (scalded but not boiled)
dry baby cereal, such as Gerber's

Cool the milk to lukewarm. Add enough dry cereal to make a "sloppy" mixture fairly thick, but still thin enough to go through a medicine dropper.

Cereal goodies. Mix the milk formula, then add enough dry baby cereal (such as Gerber's) to make a stiff, dry dough. Shape it into balls as shown in the picture and dry. Feed to baby animals being started on solid food.

146   **Nut balls.** Use the same recipe as for cereal goodies, but add 4

tablespoons of fine nut meal, usually pecan, of the kind sold for cookies and cakes. Shape and dry.

Apple Dumplings. Mix as for nut balls, but use 2 tablespoons of finely chopped raw apples as a part of the liquid. Shape and dry.

Nut balls with egg. Mix as for nut balls, adding 1 small, raw egg yolk. Feed to animals already weaned. Usually all *weaned* animals can have this formula, but if diarrhea should result, remove the egg. Be sure the nut balls with egg are *thoroughly* dried. Honey may be used instead of Karo.

When older animals refuse to take vitamins or medication prescribed by your vet, it is possible to conceal the substances in this recipe in small amounts. If using Pet Drops, add only enough to reach the first mark on the dropper which comes with the bottle.

To shape. When you have mixed a fairly stiff and dry dough, take a small portion at a time and roll it between your palms into a "rope" about as thick as a pencil. Using scissors, cut this into bits and then roll the bits into balls.

Place the balls on a greased paper or greased foil and dry them on an electric warming tray if you have one or in the sun. Do not try to dry them in the oven, as they will bake only on the outside and stay soft on the inside. They can be dried on pilot light heat without getting soft.

If you dry them out-of-doors, keep a close watch on them to make sure that bluejays or other bold birds do not carry them off.

For small animals, such as chickaree, make the balls the size of large peas. For larger animals make them the size of mothballs.   147

HOW LONG
DO WILD ANIMALS LIVE?

Animals usually live longer in captivity than in the wild. By "captivity" we mean a clean, well-managed zoo with trained people to see that they receive proper food, care, and exercise and a zoo veterinarian to treat them if they become ill. In the hands of untrained people very few wild babies survive.

In a good zoo they are protected from accidents, hunters, traps, disease, severe weather, natural enemies, and chemical sprays which may poison the food of some. Those which live in a protected state or national park probably live longer than those in the wilderness.

Naturalists agree that life in the wild is best for all animals, but do not agree on how long animals live. The figures here are only a thoughtful estimate.

Cottontail Rabbits. Some naturalists think they can live as long as 5 years in the wild. In captivity cottontails sometimes live as long as 9 years. I know a country woman who has been feeding the same cottontail for 10 years. She raised him after his mother was killed and he has never left her dooryard.

Raccoons. A raccoon is considered old at 7 years but may live as long as 12 in the wild. In captivity he may live 15 years.

I know another country woman who raised a baby raccoon whose mother was killed in highway traffic. When he was a year old, she released him in the woods. He refused to stay and kept coming back for his favorite food, corn bread. For 15 years he lived in her barn, and during that time she baked a pan of corn bread for him every day.

Groundhogs. The life of a groundhog in the wild is 4 or 5 years, naturalists think. Captives live at least that long, and some have lived to be 10 years old. Groundhogs are very good at taking care of themselves, and those raised in captivity soon adjust, almost happily, to life in the wild.

Possums. A possum seldom lives more than 2 years in the wild. Those in captivity live longer, and one was reported to have lived 7 years. The possums I have raised died quietly of old age at about 3 years.

Chickaree Squirrel. This sassy little red squirrel lives from 2–5 years in the wild and has lived as long as 9 years in captivity. Few live to be more than 3, however, even with good care.

Fox Squirrels. Most fox squirrels do not live more than 4 or 5 years in captivity, though some have lived to be 9 or 10. It is doubtful that any fox squirrel lives longer than 5 years in the wild, even when he has plenty of food and water and manages to keep away from enemies or accidents.

RELEASING YOUR ANIMAL

It is a shocking and sometimes fatal experience for any animal accustomed to being loved, petted, and sheltered to be suddenly cast out into a terrifying world away from everyone and everything familiar, even though this terrifying world is considered his native habitat.

Many people seem to think that an animal released from captivity will be so overjoyed by his new freedom that he will immediately rush into the woods and live happily ever after. Instead, any animal unprepared for freedom will be lost and panic-stricken and can come to harm almost at once.

We once had a young fox squirrel we called Geegah (Jee-jah) because her lively spirit reminded us of a little Gypsy girl by the same name. A veterinarian brought her to us for convalescent care after she had been hit by a car and suffered a concussion.

From the first we felt sure that Geegah had been in captivity because she showed no fear of people and liked being with us, which would not be true of an older squirrel from the wild. She wanted us to hold and pet her and seemed pleased and at home in her comfortable cage.

Though we could only guess, we believed she had been someone's pet. Perhaps her "owner" gave her freedom without realizing that she could get into trouble. Or was tired of taking care of her. Or was upset because Geegah had reached the age when she would naturally gnaw any nearby wood, even window-sills and furniture. Or perhaps Geegah, being clever and curious, had managed to open her cage and run away. Whatever the story, she did not know how to take care of herself and was badly hurt, almost killed.

Many people who are eager to adopt wild animal babies soon tire of them and don't want to be bothered by them. Or as the animals grow larger, they don't have room for them or can't handle them. Sometimes such people think they can solve their problem by turning the animals over to a zoo. But most zoos already have all the animals they need and want and are not pleased to be asked to take on other people's burdens. Too, *all* zoos are not *good* zoos. Many, especially small private ones, have poor facilities and inadequate quarters where the animals are dirty, neglected, half starved, and often ill treated. And they are still in captivity.

City parks, usually the second plan of people who want to get rid of their wild pets, are not a good choice either. Most of these parks already have all the wildlife they can support and are full of noise, traffic, and confusion. Nor are the animals always safe from harm by dogs or vandals.

Possums and rabbits seem to adjust most readily to wooded areas which offer shelter and streams of water. But if you release your animal on a farm, he may soon be hunted down and killed by dogs, hunters, or a natural enemy he does not know how to avoid.

We are fortunate in living in a wooded area protected from   151 dogs and hunters where our foundlings can be safely released as they grow up. Here we have observed that the more intelligent woods animals soon learn from others of their kind and adjust well to their new life *if* they are provided with food, water, and shelter until they are able to find these things for themselves.

You may not be able to do this for your animal, but you can introduce him to the out-of-doors while he is still in his cage. Though it may seem surprising, animals raised in captivity are often afraid of the very surroundings in which they should feel most at home. So take your animal in his cage (or at your side if he is used to this) to some pleasant, shaded spot on a summer day. Let him see other animals, feel the wind, listen to the leaves, hear the birds, become acquainted with the earth smells. He needs to become acquainted with night, too, and with the night sounds. But stay close to him at first, for learning to feel at home in this strange new world should be a gradual experience.

It is because animals raised in captivity often have a fear of natural things that we are so concerned for them. Thunderstorms, which terrify birds and animals raised in the wild, are twice as terrifying to those which were not. Animals new to the out-of-doors sometimes fear the touch of grass, the calls of birds, and such natural sounds as the whir of wings. Some are afraid of space and if released too suddenly will panic and run wildly into danger. There is much for them to learn, even when they are given a chance to learn it slowly, while still in your care.

An animal raised in a house or barn or other building has learned to feel secure within walls. So if he is released without the right preparation, he will probably go to the nearest house and try to get in, since he has always found friends, food, and kindness here. Or he may approach strangers, since people are the only family he has ever known. But strangers may start screaming "Rabies!" and call the police. He may be chased, shot, frightened, or beaten to death. This has happened many times.

On the other hand, if he is released in the woods or a forest far from strangers without preparation, he is still in grave danger. He has not learned how to hide from enemies or to find shelter. He may be attacked and killed or badly hurt by predators. He may be trapped or shot by hunters. He may go into shock from sheer terror.

The best solution seems to be a large state or national park where the naturalist or ranger will take a personal interest in helping you return your friend to the wild.

In Indiana this type of rehabilitation has become a state policy of the Indiana Department of Natural Resources, headed by a concerned director, Joseph D. Cloud.

Under this plan, certain of the state parks have nature centers where, by arrangement, a naturalist will receive any native wild animal raised in captivity and help him to adjust. The animal is kept at the center until he learns to know and trust his new friend. Then he ventures into the forest as he likes, but always comes back for food. Later, as he grows accustomed to the wild and overcomes his fears, he will range farther and farther from the center, eventually becoming wholly adjusted and able to live his own life.

A dedicated young naturalist at an Indiana state park, Maryanne Newsome, has had gratifying success in returning wild pets to the forest. One of her first charges was a little fawn who soon ventured away from the center but came back regularly, three times a day, for his bottle. As he grew older, he weaned himself and started living off the land but remained in the park woodlands with others of his kind.

153

Before you release your animal, try to make such an arrangement with someone in a protected area of this kind. The naturalist will tell you when to bring your animal. And while it is probably not required, it would be thoughtful to take along a supply of staple foods for him, so as not to burden the center's budget.

INDEX

Names in italics refer to specific animals